The Management "MANIFESTO"

The Management "MANIFESTO"

By
TOM CHAPMAN

A division of Squire Publishers, Inc.
4500 College Blvd.
Leawood, KS 66211
1/888/888-7696

Copyright 2002
Printed in the United States

ISBN: 1-58597-147-2

Library of Congress Control Number: 2002106807

A division of Squire Publishers, Inc.
4500 College Blvd.
Leawood, KS 66211
1/888/888-7696

CONTENTS

The Peculiar Skill Of Listening 1
Support Your Local Employee 5
Who You Calling a Pro! 9
The Word Is "Stressure" 11
Boy ... Can I Pick 'Em 14
What's So Funny? 17
Who Needs A Whole Tribe of Chiefs 20
Integrity, How Do You Spell It? 24
You Said ...What! 28
The Importance of Nurturing, Well ... Okay? 31
Cloning — It's A Gas 34
On Being Yourself 38
Did You Say People Skills? 41
The Depressed Art of Chewing Ass 43
Lonesome? Hold A Meeting 46
On My Signal, "Bonzai!" 49
Blue Skies or The Blues ... Your Call 51
Perks, Privileges & Protocol 55
Whatcha Think? 58
Altruistic ...Who, Me? 62
An Incredibly Credible Person 64
Involvement — The Final Solution 67
Some Game Plan ... "Don't Lose!" 70
"L" Is For Loyalty, Love, and Leprosy 73
Delegate or Dump? Which is it? 76
Of Course, I like You, It's just 79
The Need To Know ... Know What? 82
The Dream Team 85
Hustle, Not Necessarily A Street Word 88
Great Expectations 91
It's A Wonderful Whirl 94

DEDICATION

To Mike Lawless...A Good Friend

INTRODUCTION

THE "MANIFESTO" is a compilation of weekly articles written as a supplement to my services as Management Consultant to twenty-five individual corporations. Each article identifies one of the qualities important to lead/follow relationships. Encouraged by the enthusiastic reception of biased clients, I turned a blind eye to the hundreds of excellent volumes already written on the subject and combined them for this book. Together they provide a tongue-in-cheek but on-the-level profile of leadership in business.

Rest assured that the " Manifesto" doesn't presume to show the boss how to run his job, but instead attempts to establish a sharper appreciation for certain values, and in doing so makes a complex job easier, more palatable and fun.

I tend to view leader development with a jaundiced eye. In my view, people either have what it takes or they don't, and if they don't, there's not too damned much you can do about it. The chances of making a leader out of a follower are akin to making a jumper out of a truck-horse. A father of a good friend, an elderly Sicilian with a disarming garlic accent said it best, "If you godit, you godit. If you ain't godit, you ain't godit."

Leaders, including good ones, come plain or with amenities: personality, education, a sense of humor and a commanding voice, none of which can hurt. However, I've known some crackerjack leaders with negligible control of the language, voices like Donald Duck, and the personality of a dead fish. Amenities can be developed, but the qualities that make a difference better be there at the start or, as they say, it will be a long afternoon.

Does every quality have to be in place for a person to be a successful leader? It would be nice, but of course not. However, once they've been identified, which is the goal of the Manifesto, one can judge for themselves whether they've "godit" or better start "gedding it." The " Manifesto," by devoting an entire chapter to each, attempts to travel down the path of understanding in a manner I think you will find fun, and quite different.

In general, the word "leader," invokes images of strong jawed men making strong jawed stands or perhaps a bloodied general screaming hoarse commands from a dying horse. Damned moving! Instead, we begin our Manifesto by suggesting that learning to keep one's mouth shut and listen is the first step towards substantial leadership.

THE PECULIAR SKILL OF LISTENING

The Situation:
"No man alive would listen to one word you say if he didn't know for sure it would be his turn next."
— *Edgar Watson Howe, whoever he was.*

LEADERS INTUITIVELY UNDERSTAND the immeasurable value of careful listening. According to Woodrow Wilson, "The ear of the leader rings with the voices of the people," or, the one I like better: "Listening, not imitation, is the truest form of flattery." ... Dr. Joyce Brothers

Not paying attention to people when they speak, besides being damned rude, sends a clear message that you don't think much of them, or what they have to say. On the other hand, listening carefully, "with both ears," so to speak, exhibits respect, care and interest. To be effective as a leader (someone usually in need of followers), stop trying to impress people and start being impressed by them.

Whether you want them or not, you'll make more friends in two weeks of good listening than you will in two years of trying to convince people how smart you are. Good listeners connect with more people on more levels and develop deeper and stronger relationships than good talkers. Why? Because talkers are a dime a dozen and good listeners top everyone's "most wanted" list.

People must be heard, listen to them and you have a disciple.

If you don't listen to people, whoever they may be, you can bet your bippy they'll find someone who will. Relinquishing your role as "Speaker" is tough, but nothing will get you more response than allowing the other person to take the floor while you focus on what they're saying. And if it kills you, avoid all impulses to say something brilliant when they finish. IF IT KILLS YOU!!!

We respond and move towards those who listen to us.

Problem: As we progress in business we're inclined to listen less and talk more, thus our importance, the thing we've worked so hard for, becomes our downfall. Fascinated by the sound of our voice and infinite wisdom, we forget that we got where we are by listening and learning. So, no matter if it's the dullest human being you've ever met, someone incapable of saying one word you want to hear — shut up and listen! With this act of social nobility, harp music will fill the room and the hallowed mantle of leadership will descend upon your shoulders.

If you consistently listen to others, and value what they have to say, they will develop a strong loyalty to you.

Perhaps your leadership position is secure, but to assure there will be no glitches, tip-toe through the problems below for a broader understanding of the narrow path ahead.

Some barriers to good listening, like you didn't have enough already.
- The inability to focus on what's being said. (No matter how interesting)

- Mental Fatigue. (Started with the first word out of their mouth)
- Stereotyping thus pre-empting the speaker. (fun-fun-fun)
- Preoccupation with "self." (Devastating but why not)

Listening Skills
- Look at the speaker, in fact, stare. (Be sure to change directions should he move.)
- Don't interrupt. (Not easy ... not easy at all)
- Focus to understand what's being said:
  a. Listen carefully for understanding (Yours, not theirs)
  b. Listen for the message behind the message. (Very tricky)
  c. Listen for content and feeling. (Sexy n'est-ce pas)
  d. Listen with your eyes. (You know what I mean)
  e. Listen for what they're not saying. (So, say it already.)
  f. Listen with acceptance, don't prejudge. (Killjoy)
  g. Listen as you would want to be listened to. (Impossible)
- Try to determine the speaker's needs. (A better vocabulary maybe)
- Suspend judgment. (Why? At least it shows you've been listening.)
- Sum up quickly at major intervals. (Try this one without listening.)
- Ask questions. (Especially if you know the answers)
- Make listening your priority. (What else?)

The question every boss is afraid to ask: "Do people respect me and want to work for me?" Who knows? However, your chances are better once you've learned to listen. Listening builds respect, response and a following. Everyone needs to be needed; listening to them fills much of that need.

For one entire day, try listening with exaggerated attention to everyone who speaks to you, and watch as they come to life before your eyes. You'll find it an experiment you'll want to repeat.

No matter how important you may be, or how

difficult it be, by listening to someone carefully, you have made a friend.

Too, by giving others a shot at the podium, at least that amount of time spent communicating will be informative. Though hard to accept at first, listening to anyone will make you smarter, and because you do, people will gather round you like the flowers in a bouquet.

SUPPORT YOUR LOCAL EMPLOYEE

"Flatter me, and I may not believe you. Criticize me, and I may not like you. Ignore me, and I may not forgive you. Encourage me, and I will not forget you.
...William A Ward

VOLUMES HAVE BEEN WRITTEN about the need for S&E, "Support and Encouragement," in the leadership role. The following is our contribution.

For anyone carrying the burdens of leadership, S&E represents one of its more pleasant aspects; after all, what can be more satisfying than helping someone reach their goal. There's little question that support and encouragement makes a difference; the problem is how to go about delivering the merchandise.

"How To" books on the subject have the intellectual punch of the "See Jack run" series: "See Jack frown. See Jack's supervisor pat Jack on the po-po. See Jack smile!" The "pat on the po-po" is the NFL version of S&E.

We'll be more efficient as leaders once we accept that although the perfect employee doesn't exist, with support and encouragement those we have can become better than they are. My years have convinced me that new employees will seldom make it to ground level unless management busts its buns to get them there.

S&E comes in all shapes and sizes; for instance, lending money. New employees, like most relatives, are usually short of cash and may turn to the boss (you) for help. Who else can they turn to, relatives? Hah! Should it happen someone needs money, and it will happen, handling the situation calls for a special "loan" mentality. Let me explain:

Example 1: Employee "X" needs money; both her parents were killed in a Luge accident, her brother is in a mental institution, her sister has run off with a polo player, the cat needs a kidney transplant and they're about to repossess her car. What do you do — give her advice? I don't think so. Like it or not, you are about to be asked for money, a situation that needs fast evaluation: how much will she need ... how much do you need her ... will you comply or suggest she join her brother.

Loaning money to employees is never an attractive option, but if it's a valuable employee or at least a cute one, you'll probably wind up doing it. Refusing the loan would be the wisest option, but you probably won't do that. So, keeping in mind that you'll probably never get it back, how much are you prepared to give? What really matters is that handled poorly, even making the loan can alienate the employee forever.

The role calls for character: 1. Don't ask her how she got in this condition! 2. Don't moralize about seldom making loans! 3. Don't tell picture stories about getting stuck like this before! 4. Don't ask how she's going to pay you back! JUST GIVE HER THE DAMNED MONEY! Put through all that other stuff and you may as well say "No" because she'll hate you anyway.

This is a chance for you to be a hero, so don't screw up! Once you've decided to give her the money — bite the bullet; give up the earthly pleasures of rubbing it in ... do it nicely, let her off the hook, shell out like the gracious SOB you've always dreamed of being. Do it nicely, let her feel good about herself — she'll adore you. Asking for a loan is tough, almost as tough as making one. Which would you rather do?

Before going to number two, let's see where we are. This is the S&E potion of the "Leadership" series, "support and encouragement," the business of shoring up the spirits in your charge. You wanted to be a boss, a leader, well, this is a great place to start so ... start.

Example 2. It's been a bad week at the store and you're short of money. Bills are overdue and the IRS is no longer smiling. However, you're not concerned because you're expecting a big sale. Unfortunately, the prospect decides he prefers the BMW instead. How did this happen to you? Probably the person closing the sale was ineffective.

Depressed and worried, you want to shoot him. Well, you can't shoot him, people don't shoot closers nowadays. However, unless you do something about him, he'll go home and shoot himself. Worse than that, he might not

It's at times like these that any leadership laying around will surface. Instead of responding instinctively and maiming the man, you tell him with forced enthusiasm that his presentation was great, and for the life of you, you can't understand why the prospect didn't buy! The idea is to send him home feeling good about himself or at least better. God it's hard but ... that's SUPPORT, and no one ever said it was easy.

On second thought ... screw leadership, fire him ... make you feel better.

Praising successful performances is easy, everyone's on a high and back-slapping is fun and good exercise. Following a successful sale, applause is unnecessary icing and the employee thinks to himself,: "Why don't they come around when I need them, when I'm doing badly?" Praising a failing performance takes character. True leadership is offering praise when every bone in your body is screaming for revenge! It's only when people stumble that a little affection means something.

Unfortunately, it's the nature of the management beast. When someone screws up and really needs our support, we react to the results and fail to supply emotional needs. At times like these, we have the thinking capacity of a sloth.

To do their best, staff needs employer approval, but it cannot be based on successful performance only. The ability to see an employee objectively and with affection for their efforts floats a boss above the crowd. Appreciating effort rather than results takes class. Generously offering encouragement and support in moments of emotional need canonizes an employer and doesn't cost the company a cent.

Our sphere of influence may be limited but it exists and we must do with it what we can. The human spirit responds with fierce emotion to anyone who acknowledges their role and appreciates what they try to do regardless of how well they may do it.

WHO YOU CALLING A PRO?

"What's your profession young man?"
"I'm a bum, sir."
"You call that a profession?"
"Absolutely, sir. According to a leading psychologist, someone making a living doing what other people do for a hobby is correct in calling themselves a professional. After all, people are paid to take part in sports, are they not? And, is it not a fact that artists, dancing teachers, golfers and hookers are professionals?"

"As for me," he concluded, "where some people bum around for the fun of it, I do it for a living. Ergo, I am a professional."

TAKING THIS PHILOSOPHY into consideration, whether management per se can be called a "profession" is an easy call. The activities parallel those of a vacation: sitting (rest & relaxation), beau coup trips to the bathroom (exercise), constant staff supervision (people watching), extensive letter writing (wish you were here) and group discussions (playing bingo). Note also that they're not very professional in appearance, seem moderately content and appear to have a fair amount of walk-around money.

"Pro" has other meanings as well. For example, regardless of your calling, nothing falls more pleasantly on the ears than "... Now, THERE'S A REAL PRO!" With these words you are now rated as a professional, "top dog," "numero uno," "the Man!" How fine. The question remains, how do you get the rating?

If the word "pro" is in reference to management ability, qualifying should require a strong presence of "know-how." Knowledgeable management is the backbone staff needs to function properly. Management "know-how" supplies this. This is never more evident than in sports where a team's confidence in coaching decisions makes a major difference in the way they perform.

The ability to inspire runs a close second. Without inspiration, the "ordinary" prevails. Unless staff is inspired, it will have difficulty making it to ground level, let alone excelling. Though inspiration alone may not make a staff great, it's the fuel on which it feeds. Inspiration changes work to pleasure, but how to inspire? Perhaps by doing things as they should be done and being the person a boss should be, by being a mentor and role model, by being a leader in the true sense of the word. Treating staff as you would family is a start, because in the final analysis they'll do more for you than family ever would.

For management to receive a "pro" rating it must be able to provide financial success for its workers. An employee will kill for the employer who is truly concerned about them. Unfortunately, the average employer's concern is for the company and themselves; the employer who places staff interests on a par with their own is a rare bird. Of course, unless the company is successful, everyone winds up with "bupkers" (Yiddish for nothing or was it large breasts). So, regardless how high sounding your plans for your employees are, unless the company makes it, it's all talk.

Webster on Profession: *An avowal, a declaration.*

Webster on Professional: *A person who does work of the highest standard*

Webster on Professionalism: *Being of professional quality.*

THE WORD IS "STRESSURE"

THE STATE OF MENTAL FLUX most closely associated with leadership is "stress, "but as my sainted, eighty-year-old Kansas City Russian immigrant landlord, Israel Bettinger, would have asked, "Tell me vy?" And though I'm not sure "vy," I am sure that stress exists and in varying sizes, large sizes being emotionally based and small ones, more than likely, indigestion.

Contrary to what we think, stress, although responsibility related, is optional. The same set of circumstances can cause varying amounts of stress, sometimes none at all, depending on the *stressee*. The simplest of work requirements drive some people bananas, while others die of boredom with problems fit for an Einstein.

The first definition of "stress" in Webster's big book is one we're all acquainted with:

> *"To make something important, by stressing it."*

The second definition is equally familiar once we know what the damned words mean:

> *"An action on a body by any system of balanced forces, whereby strain or deformation results,"*

Which brings to mind some of the more deformed souls I've worked with. The third is a nice little throwaway:

> *"The ratio of force to area."*

The fourth and fifth are real grabbers:

> *"Any stimulus such as fear or pain that disturbs or interferes with normal physiological equilibrium."*

And finally,

> *Physical, mental or emotional strain or tension.*

So, according to the word man, the executive we think of as "stressed out!" has actually: placed too much importance on his work, thus creating an imbalance of inner forces (deformation), the fear of which they must face as well as the pain of taking care of it. The side effects are emotional strains and tensions. Some one should have pulled the plug.

However, first we must agree that stress, is self-inflicted:

> *Not one damn thing in the world is stressful unless you choose to make it so*   ... TC

The next important cause of emotional imbalances in executives is something we call "pressure," another emotion of choice and certainly the basis for stress. For example, "deadlines," big on a long list of pressure points, but only if one decides that the deadline absolutely has to be made. If making the "deadline" is optional, the "pressure" disappears. A fleeting suggestion of screw it, and you're home free.

Back to Webster, this time on "Pressure":

> *The exertion of a force upon a surface by an ob-*

ject ... the state of being compressed ... harassment: oppression; the pressures of daily life ... a state of trouble or embarrassment ... A CONSTRAINING OR COMPELLING FORCE OR INFLUENCE ... urgency, as of affairs or business ... (affairs or business hmmmmm) ... to force towards a particular end — a big money deal perhaps?

So, we have Joe Executive who presumably has: 1. Some sort of force being exerted on his mind which is 2. Pressing him into a state of troubled embarrassment, as well as compelling, influencing and forcing him towards taking a nap, or possibly stealing company pencils.

Problems as similar as pressure and stress can be confusing, so I've combined them into one compelling, forceful, nonsense word ... "Stressure." Neat?

Here's a quote by someone I'd love to have known personally, someone who obviously learned to deal with his/her "stressures." With a few words he places everything in perspective:

"MY DECISION IS "MAYBE." AND THAT'S FINAL.

If I've managed to plant even a seed of doubt regarding the reality of "stress," or "pressure" ... good. These executive-type emotional cop-outs are in reality a measure of one's acceptance of responsibilities. Someone really stressed out has taken his position too seriously. He/she, cares ... too much.

This is bad?

BOY — CAN I PICK 'EM

WADAYA MEAN he quit! Yagoddabee kidding! WadayaMEAN without notice! YaMEAN he's gone! He said I'm a WHAT! And after all I did for him? Stop his last check!

If there's any part of running a business that gets you right in the heart burn, it's the business of hiring, firing and training, the difficulty of which lies in repetition that demands the patience of a saint. As management consultant for twenty years, I'll venture the problems of personnel acquisition and maintenance sends more company heads to psychiatrists than their wives, girlfriends or bookies.

Large corporations cop out by employing a Personnel Manager. In "days of Yore," this was the food taster, the poor sod who ate the poison first so the king could enjoy a more deserving death. Personnel managers assure that companies will acquire sufficient high quality personnel and a payroll to match. This they do with the help of expensive ads, sign-on bonuses, corporate perks, fringe benefits and posh working situations. Things most small businessmen would love to have for themselves.

> *Among the chief worries of today's executives is the large number of unemployed still on the payroll.*

Small companies are lucky if they can offer paid vacations and sometimes, not even that. Not being able to match the big boys confines them to the tail end of the employment chain; they can't outbid the heavy weights and it would be foolish to try. How can one-inch classified ads compete with fifteen and twenty-inch display ads offering BMW's with personalized license plates. The catch is that the applicant has to be able to write their name without referring to notes.

If you're a small company, your approach to the work force should be your pride in being a small company, "Because you are small, you are unique!" Being small should be the attraction. Maybe you're not rich, but you are special. Your slogan, "We can't give you a BMW, but we give you love," as well as, "Grow with the company!"

- An individualized training program
- Large areas of responsibility & recognition
- Participation in company decisions and futures
- Programs for personalized growth and futures.

With a clearly worded ad using the above emotional appeals in classified on Sunday, by noon Monday you'll probably have received calls from one or two IBM rejects that either couldn't spell their name without notes or thought a BMW was a physic.

Collecting good people takes time and thought; after all, you're competing with the big boys ,which can be done, but it isn't easy! Know what? You'll succeed because people, whoever they may be, want the same things, and money is just one of them. People want money, recognition, attention, acceptance and love, and employees, regardless of what you may think of them personally, are people!

The things small companies offer that big ones can't are: involvement, interaction and relationships — much too troublesome for large corporations. Besides, people are afraid of large companies, a fear of getting lost in the shuffle, of losing their identity, or worse, not existing at all. All very real.

So, let's say we're successful and attract applicants — who will we hire, who will we reject, what do we want? We're not going to get the pick of the crop, they'll go to companies with more to offer, but, don't despair, we'll get our share, and when we do, we'll need decisions. Barnes and Noble offers a selection of books on every aspect of hiring personnel, perhaps intended for large companies, but buy one anyway.

One thing for sure: a small company can't reject applicants because they don't look or smell right. Your needs and the scarcity of applicants dictate you consider every applicant carefully and that you look at them differently. You cannot afford the luxury of rejecting applicants on the basis of "appearance," whether it be dress or physical. That "you can't tell a book by it's cover" is never more true then when it applies to applicants. Beneath that cheap suit, bad complexion and missing tooth may beat the heart of the best employee you ever had. Only time and patience will tell.

Reject no one without careful consideration unless they've urinated in reception and then, give it a lot of thought!

It's your call, as the owner you is da *man!* The decision to hire, train and spend is yours to make. Good or bad, you're going to be stuck with them, so go at it like you knew what you were doing; long and short form questionnaires, multiple interviews, biographical surveys, the Full Monte. After a few months of busting your buns training and supporting them, you'll know the truth ... either you have yourself an employee or you've added one more nightmare to your tax contribution. If you discover another way ... my address is in the book.

If hard work were such a wonderful thing, surely the rich would have kept it all to themselves.
— *Lane Kirkland, Pres. CIO-AFL*

WHAT'S SO FUNNY?

THE PROBLEM with having a sense of humor, and there are several, is knowing when to leave it alone. Leaders with a sense of humor need a strong sense of decorum. Whether humor works for you will depend on knowing when to keep your humorous mouth shut. There are times humor works, and others when Billy Crystal couldn't get a smile. Sure, everyone loves to laugh, but not all the time and certainly not at themselves. If your humor is at someone else's expense, you can bet there's one person who won't think it's funny, and eventually that may be you.

Too, when cozying up to people in a humorous vein, you had best know what they think is funny. Poking fun at something someone is fond of or getting a laugh at their expense can lose you a friend, or worse, an employee.

> *A difference in taste in jokes, is a great strain on the affections.*
>
> George Elliot...Daniel Debonda

Working hard to be funny simply isn't worth it. People may appreciate that you're trying to make them feel good, but it may also make them uncomfortable. The laughs you get may be a release of stress rather than a sign of enjoyment. Speakers with a good connection to their audience ordinarily receive generous response even for bad humor. So, don't be concerned about the humor, be concerned about the connection.

As a leader you'll do a lot of talking, it goes with the territory; however, be careful that in the process you don't start thinking of yourself as funny. A little humor every now and then is fine, but because you're in front of an audience doesn't make you a stand-up comic. Refrain from telling jokes. Neil Simon, one of the world's funniest men, claims he has never listened to or told a joke. According to Mr. Simon, any direct effort to be funny is a trip you'll never finish.

> **Men show their character in nothing more clearly than by what they think laughable.**
> ...*Wolfgang von Goethe*

"The secret source of humor," according to Mark Twain, "is not joy, but sorrow." Little wonder then that bosses have better senses of humor than workers. Originally I thought that because bosses had more money than workers they were happier. What bosses really have more of is headaches and they're not terribly funny. If you find there are two office parties being thrown simultaneously, one for bosses and one for workers, go to the one for workers, you'll have more fun. Besides they're younger and better looking.

> *F.M. Colby, in "Satire and Teeth," claims,* **Men will confess to murder, arson, treason, false teeth and a wig, before they'll admit to not having a sense of humor.**

Too, according to the author Sinclair Lewis, There are two insults no human being will endure: that he has no sense of humor and that he has never known trouble.

People lacking humor usually take themselves too seriously, considering everything they do or say to be important, but we know better, don't we? On the other hand, the ability to laugh at one's self will see you through some pretty impossible situations.

Listening to a popular speaker, I polled a few of the ladies in the audience to see what it was they liked about him. Most said they liked him because he seemed so "vulnerable." Not strong, although he was, not funny, which he was, not interesting and he was, but ... because he "seemed vulnerable." Maybe it was a feminine thing, but for them he was very human.

Human ... humor? Probably some crazy Latin derivative.

In the end you will be regarded by the way you affect others, by how you make them feel. So, be the boss, be strong, be a leader, but don't forget the human thing. People have to sense something in your make-up, a humanity, a desire to enjoy life and a need to share that enjoyment with them. Empathizing, I think they call it.

WHO NEEDS A WHOLE TRIBE OF CHIEFS?

LISTENING to Anwar Sadat, President of Egypt, complain about his congress and the extent of illiteracy in his country, Ben Gurion, President of Israel, commented, "Stop complaining, how would you like to be president in a country full of presidents?"

Whether it be sports, business or government, everyone involved can be slotted in one of three categories which for simplification we will refer to as: Number "Ones," "Twos" and "Threes." Although completely different in character all three are bound together by their shared goal; to make a living! Only their personal raison d'etre, separates them.

Number Ones. The idea people, the thinkers and entrepreneurs without whom little happens. Without their spirit of innovation and change, growth of any kind ceases to exist. Number Ones have the imagination, courage and confidence to create and promote. They are the "leaders," people with the capacity to inspire, motivate, raise capital and turn thought into action.

Number Twos. This group seldom has an idea they can verbalize. Generally hard workers, their minds are busy doing what they've been told. BUT! ... Show them what you want them to do, put them in the driver's seat, and then get out of the way! Number Twos can take ideas and make them work, but don't leave out the details, especially if they're imaginative ones.

Number Threes. These are the Indians, the tribe you can't do without, the workers. So busy working, they seldom pop with an idea, and if they had one, putting it to work might blow a fuse. They know little about motivation except as it might apply to their check. Impeccable work habits make them the most satisfactory group to deal with. Their philosophy; "Tell me what you want done, tell me when you want it done, tell me how you want it done, tell me how long you want me to do it, and when I'm done, pay me for it. Just don't tell me WHY you want it done, it's none of my business."

When a number three stops thinking like this, they're on their way to becoming a number two or even a "one."

So what? No one goes around looking for numbered people, "Sorry, no ideas please, you're a number two." However, once we can learn to appreciate their distinctly different capabilities and how to use them, leadership problems start to disappear.

By identifying these capabilities early on, we can also avoid wasting time trying to make silk purses out of sow's ears, and, vice versa. Should a sow want to be a silk purse, then let it be on her own head, in which case she'll soon exchange her sty for a penthouse. On the other hand, if the change is something we promote and not the sow, we may wind up sharing the sty.

When we attempt to transplant our own desires and capabilities into others in some vainglorious attempt to change or remold them, we're in trouble. Usually we do this sort of thing because, being fond of them, we want "more" for them. Unfortunately, instead of a successful cloning we make them miserable. People perform better within their own capabilities, and until these develop, there isn't much anyone can do.

You may change what people want, but whether changing their ability to get it is a questionable endeavor.

The great Tommy Armour wrote a book called "How to Play Your Best Golf," in which he makes the sensible claim that "not everyone can be a champion." BUT, he says, anyone can rise above the crowd by honing what talents they have. In this way the prospects of becoming a happy achiever rather than a psychotic failure are favorable.

The workers, or number "Threes," are the warriors of the business world, the front line, the offense and defense. Without these trained personnel, the most promising company is helpless. Warriors working comfortably within the zone of their expertise will play "Their Best Golf." If they are overachievers with extensive ability, remaining a number "three" will be impossible. Eventually they will have to assume their rightful place in the hierarchy.

As for finding them, well, that's the rub. In today's market place, ones, twos or threes are all like hen's teeth, although not in equal degrees of scarcity. With patience one can eventually accumulate a sufficient number of warriors (number threes). Progressive acquisition programs and sharp management should be more than able to build the tribe to a fighting force.

Number "Twos" will evolve from your "Threes." Mid-level management, (Number "Twos") have never been a problem. At least I've never found it to be. Strong warriors (male or female) offer great potential for mid-level management.

Number "Ones" ... well, that's a different story. In sixty years of interviewing staff, I can count on three hands the true number "Ones" I've met. As to how many I've developed ... none. Either they were number "Ones" when we met or forget it. I may have rounded off a few rough edges, but did I actually develop a number "One" — no. Fortunately, we don't need many "ones," but those we have make everything possible.

A secret! HIRE AND TRAIN ONE STAFF MEMBER AT A TIME!!! GOOD PEOPLE DON'T COME IN BUNCHES.

The ability to hire train and maintain personnel, stimulate thought and move them towards success — this is what number "ones" are all about. Hopefully, we're speaking about you.

INTEGRITY? HOW DO YOU SPELL IT?

IN A LEADERSHIP POSITION, how you are "known" may garner more support than what you do. By the same token, how you are "known" can make things tough. So ... how should one want to be known?

For starters, you certainly want to be known as a person of integrity, a curiously impressive word. Its many meanings include: truthful, caring, reliable, dependable, trustworthy, fair, sincere, forthright, open, square, faithful, just, etc., etc., etc. Outside of yourself, how many people do you know that fit that description?

Because of the scarcity of this commodity in today's society, a little integrity goes a long way; even a smidgen of it under your finger nails is outstanding.

Identifying leadership qualities is difficult — like colognes, the characteristics of the scent changes depending on who's wearing it. For example, authority, a must asset for leadership, when wielded by different people, manifests itself quite differently. To "lead" effectively, one must certainly be authoritative, but what does that mean? Authority can be either a commanding force or little more than a personal influence. Every leader lends their own interpretation to the word. You can bet the farm, however, that:

Authority in any form will be resisted unless wielded by a person of integrity.

So, are you a person of integrity? I suppose to an extent we all are, the difference being what percentage of the stuff we lay claim to? One hundred percent? I don't think so. One hundred percent means you declare everything going through customs — your tax return is squeaky clean, not even one fudge. How about those little things we do when we're certain no one will find out? No, one hundred percent is too much to ask, and it's not important.

I think of integrity as being the way we handle things affecting others, particularly the people who work for us. In their excellent book, "Becoming a Person of Influence," Maxwell and Doran say, "Integrity commits itself to character, over gain"... "people over gain"... "people over things"... "principle over convenience." Philip Brooks, a 19th century clergyman once said, and I love it:

"Character is made in the small moments of our lives."

One test of character lies in our knee-jerk response to temptation For example, how would you respond if an employee from another company, who for reasons of their own, wants to come dance with you, and leave the guy who brung him — the one who supported him through the non-productive period of his employment, the poor sod who is still waiting to get some of his investment back.

What you do with this sort of temptation says a lot about your integrity and style, or the lack of it. Actually, you could get away with anything; after all, you didn't solicit him, you're home free except for your sense of integrity. Having integrity isn't a fun thing, it's a bear unless, like me, you're a naturally wonderful person.

Integrity is an inside job, one of those damned qualities that isn't determined by people or circumstances. Excellent credentials, great wealth, knowledge or exceptional capabilities are real nice but they have nothing to do with integrity. A person can have it all and still be a putz. By the same token, they can have minus assets and be a person of integrity.

An integrity check for employers:

1. Would you fire an employee with equal dispatch if they were a personal friend?
2. A good sales prospect shows up. Would you hand it over to a weak salesman who was "up" or bring in a hot hand? I'll never tell.
3. In dealing with the above mentioned applicant who wanted to switch companies, would you: A. Call the other company and tell them what's happening? B. Suggest he go back to his boss and straighten out his problems. C. Hire him and keep your mouth shut. All three at different times maybe?
4. How long would it take you to hire a great salesman who has a record of over-imbibing, or bothering the ladies? Would it depend on how great and what ladies?
5. Would you be inclined to fire an undesirable employee before or after vacation? Unfair question?

These may be common problems, but the decisions become uncommon when a little integrity enters the picture.

Integrity means paying bills on time, living up to your word, not talking behind anyone's back, donating to charities anonymously — things others assume we do, and they should mind their own business! Know-how will carry you for awhile, but eventual success will be determined not so much by what you know as by how you are known.

Albert Camus said, **Integrity has no need of rules.**

Not so short or to the point is John McDonald's great lines from "The Turquoise Lament":

"Integrity is not a conditional word. It doesn't blow in the wind or change with the weather. It is your inner image of yourself, and if you look in there and see a man who won't cheat, then you know he never will."

YOU SAID ... WHAT!

A LARGE PART of leadership talent is saying the right thing at the right time. It makes sense then, that once we've made it to the top, the less we open our mouths, the better our chances are of staying there.

Effective leaders, like all good communicators, encourage an exchange of ideas in the workplace. The best opportunities for these are staff meetings, where top management avoids the counter-productive effect of talking too much. The measure of a good meeting is the amount of audience involvement; well-placed questions and opinion searching that stimulates open debate. If management dominates the flow, they will be clueless as to what effect their meeting is having, or whether the audience had spiritually departed after lunch.

Knowing when to talk and when to shut up will come once we realize that what we say makes a difference. Unfortunately, we are not fully aware of the effect we have on others. Once we realize that, as leaders, what we say is important, the quality of our offerings will improve. Unfortunately, as we progress, more is expected of us and fulfilling our promise becomes more difficult. Because of the growing pressure to succeed, speaking, just because there's an opportunity to do so, is foolish.

Meetings provide the best opportunities to build relationships and foster team spirit, opportunities we sometimes sacrifice in our need to play "King of the Hill," hogging the floor in a silly attempt to impress our audience. Another opportunity wasted.

> ***If you confine the meeting to the sound of your own voice, you may well be the only one listening.***

Leaders are never more imposing than when they are silent. Silence is enormously commanding, in some strange way imparting a sense of wisdom. It also keeps oratorical weaknesses under wraps. Besides, letting the other guy speak, especially a subordinate, reeks of character; how generous, how grand, how confident, how smart!

To whom do we look for confidence? Doctors, certainly. Attorneys are overloaded with the stuff. Teachers, of course. Most importantly, we look to the boss, the person who controls our lifeline. Lack of confidence in this important person clouds our vision of the future, goals become suspect and efforts weaken. Leaders can easily shake staff confidence, by appearing to lose their own.

Being only human, people love the sound of their own voices, and, like this article, are apt to become a little long-winded. Contrary to Tiny Tim's claim that "You are what you eat," you are what you say. So, play it cool, and start developing the comfortable security of silence.

A Beginner's List of Communication "No-no's"
- Never: Talk business when you've had a drink. You'll never believe what you said.
- Talk about anyone behind their back. Gotta be a bloody saint.
- Exaggerate, it will return to haunt you. Especially if it's about money.
- Present things inaccurately. Employees will eat it up.
- Air personal problems. Statistics show 80% are delighted you have them

- Talk over or down to people. Unless, you want to get rid of them
- Be defensive, self protective. Just cry.
- Make excuses. Even if you have one.
- Overstate your case. Unless you're not convinced yourself
- Hog the floor. Yawn
- Lecture or posture. Who needs it.
- Argue publicly or loudly. The ugly American
- Insist on being right! Especially when you suspect you're not.
- Have an answer for everything. Gosh all hemlock but you're smart.
- Tell jokes or long winded unrelated anecdotes. Unless they're about yourself
- Just be quiet, it's easier and they'll love ya.

THE IMPORTANCE OF NURTURING? WELL, OKAY.

THE PROBLEM of converting the average applicant to a staff member, besides being complicated, can be a drag on the spirit. Grasping at wisdom we say things like, "What's worth having is worth nurturing."

As bosses, leaders of men, entrepreneurs *magnifique*, we cannot be discouraged by what seems an endless project. If not careful, we can waste a lot of time wondering why young people don't respond to leadership because, for the most part, they don't, and for the most part there isn't any. I would like to think the lack of response is a trend, but I'm afraid not, and treating it as such is wishful, stupid and dangerous. This is the way they are and this is the way they will probably stay, so ignore it and do your job.

Comparing today's staff with staffs of yesterday is frustrating and foolish! Young people today don't want what we wanted. Whether that makes them better or worse isn't the point; the point is that they're what we've got.

In search of the loyal, grateful, houseboy staff member you used to be? Good luck, they don't exist. In need of good staff today, prepare to work at it; the shoe is on the other foot — you're the houseboy, so do the job and with a little class, please.

Of course, obstacles of our own making exist like an ego? Just when you think you're doing fine, there it is, staring at you like some big bug. That egos abide in everyone is okay as long as they aren't disproportionate to the talent. The worst case for egos is that they cause us to focus on ourselves rather than staff, and the nurturing process goes belly up.

Egos tend to make "bosses" of us rather than leaders.

"Generosity — the earmark of leadership."
*And according to FAG Steven's in "Reflections and Maxims," "**Leaders give assistance, not advice.**"*

Filling a leadership role requires nurturing and assistance. Authority may get you obedience, but in the process you may lose that which you need the most, the desire of others to please you.

Then again, why should people want to please you? Probably because you've cared enough to nurture them. Webster says, to nurture is to nourish — to rear, which pretty well defines our jobs as leaders. By performing these caring acts we create the response necessary to affect leadership.

Who feeds the dog becomes its master.

When you recognize employee emotions as important, you answer an innermost hunge, a need to be loved, considered and cared for — at that point, you're on your way to leadership. Pretty heady stuff.

It is here that we separate the leaders from the boys. To succeed, an employee must believe they are worthwhile and that you value their opinion. Accomplishing this as an owner is terribly important, not because the opinion may have value but because you have valued the person who offered it. A real bear. Is it patronizing? Sure smells like it, but maybe not. Patronizing is the same as tolerating and leaders don't tolerate people, they value them, or at least that's what the good book says.

Maybe this will help. When we fail to listen to or to appreciate what people offer us, we become unreachable. An offering is an offering; if nothing comes out of it, what have we lost by paying attention? Would we have been better off if they hadn't spoken at all or we hadn't listened? How can you not be ahead of the game if you listen and by listening have nurtured?

There's little question that nurturing is beneficial, but it has its down side —— the risk of dependency. In nurturing, care must be taken to not create emotional dependency. Whatever we do for people has to be a genuine contribution to growth, not a placebo. We nurture to remove fear, establish confidence and security, and hope it pays off. You need dependents like a hole in your head. Nurturing is intended to develop character, not children.

The goal of nurturing is to develop adequate, functioning, independent beings — people you have helped to become the person they wanted to be, not the person you wanted them to be.

Leadership takes many forms, and caring enough to nurture people is certainly one of them. Mike Lawless, president of fifteen corporations, member of Mensa and a truly brilliant businessman, once said:

__To provide capable and during leadership, you must be a genuinely selfless person.__"

I'm certain he was referring to such items as empathy and nurturing.

__Start with good people, lay out the rules, communicate with your employees, motivate them and reward them. If you do all those things effectively, you can't miss__
... Lee Iococca 1924

CLONING, IT'S A GAS

> *"You can teach what you know, but you can only reproduce what you are."*

THE ABOVE QUOTE from Maxwell and Dornan's "Becoming a Person of Influence" may be true, but it doesn't go down easily. There's something unsettling about "things in our own Image" — a little God-like. Later on they qualify the message by suggesting that reproducing in our "own image" is okay, providing we clean up our act before running copies. So much for Bill Tilden who said, "If it ain't broke, don't fix it," which I'm beginning to think was the only thing he ever said, like instead of "hello."

Regardless of possible complications — as committed leaders and trainers, cloning is what we're all about. Whether in pursuit of company growth or a lack of anything better to do, we are devoted to turning staff into what we think they should be, which, with no malice intended, is a reproduction of ourselves. Ask a blindfolded artist to draw a face, and he'll draw his own, the face he sees when he closes his eyes. When we train, we reproduce what we see with our mind's eye ... ourselves.

> *A man can seldom, very seldom — fight a winning fight against his training, the odds are too heavy.*   *... Mark Twain*

If there were an option, we might do well to take advantage of it, but I didn't see what it could be until I read "Becoming A Person of Influence," in which it rationalizes that reproducing myself may be something I can't avoid, but I can make it right by becoming more worthy of copies.

But how? How to know what needs improvement? I may spot the smallest blemish, blackhead or nasal hair on someone else at fifty paces, but a metaphorical carbuncle on the end of my own nose would go unnoticed. Personal failings belong to the other guy. Self-evaluation is generally confined to questionnaires in *Cosmopolitan* as to whether my sex partner is getting her proper share of things, the results of which I refuse to discuss. Determining whether our leadership efforts are making a difference is something we won't find in *Cosmopolitan,* too bad.

Arthur Murray, the one genius I was fortunate to work with, said and firmly believed:

"Training is our most valuable asset."

Having the temerity to improve on genius, I suggest that he should have said, "Self-training is our most valuable asset." We spend our time searching for smart people, which is fine; however, we might do better by looking for people with a capacity and desire to learn.

Do you find yourself repeating something so many times that you're sick of it? My thing is, "People don't want to think — they're either too lazy or too stupid." Da da dee da da. That it happens to be true doesn't help. Suggesting that people use both sides of their brain is tantamount to offering them a bite of HIV positive cake. It seems the idea that anything worthwhile will be derived from improving their minds is incomprehensible.

The quality of a person's life is in direct proportion to their commitment to excellence, regardless of their chosen field. ...Vince Lombardi

Try this simple test: describe the perfect executive beginning with: "A perfect executive is one who," then when you've finished, ask yourself if you fit the mold. Would you give you the job? Or, you might ask yourselves the following:

1. Am I a people-person? Do people trust me? Confide in me? Want to please me? Respect me? If not, what will I do about it?

2. Do I have all the technical knowledge I need? If not, etc., etc.
3. How much experience can I claim? Success in various positions? Number of years for one employer or if self-employed how long at one endeavor? Earnings?
4. Am I a fighter, a competitor? How can I tell?
5. Have I developed patience?
6. How much have I improved in the last five years? Sales know-how? Training know-how? People know-how? Anything? Any new ideas?
7. What personal development projects am I presently involved in? Anything?
8. Name one or two personal growth books I've read in two years? Anything?
9. What releases, important memos or staff papers have I written? Anything?
10. Am I sufficiently positive...selfless...enthusiastic...fun? Anything?

The above "DO I, AM I, HAVE I" list should help you decide whether cloning yourself would be as worthwhile as, let's say, collecting stamps?

Leadership experts Warren Dennis and Bert Nanus address the issue thusly:

"It's the capacity to develop and improve their skills that distinguish leaders from followers."

Albert Schweitzer, takes a different tack:

"The great secret of success is to go through life like someone who never got used to it."

The consensus being that recharging gives you cloning rights. Remember your high school teachers, the ones who haven't recharged since they got their diplomas. They're memorable because so little about them is memorable. What we remember about them is how ineffective and boring they were, which is how we may be remembered unless we do something about it.

ON BEING YOURSELF

PROBABLY THE TOUGHEST ROLE to play in a leadership position is that of yourself. In fact, serious doubt exists whether the real "you" appears anywhere in life except in the bathroom. Anyone seeing themselves as "natural" leader is hallucinatory.

Anything the matter with that? I don't think so! Show me the person dealing with people who relies on their own sweet unadorned self to do the job, and I'll show you someone about to go into another line of work.

Dining out in Scottsdale many years ago, I was seated at a table next to Governor Barry Goldwater of Arizona having dinner with his family. I found him fascinating, not because he was fascinating, but because he was absolutely devoid of personality, probably one of the dullest celebrities I've ever eavesdropped. Governor of the State, owner of a successful department store chain, candidate for President of the United States, and his one contribution to the conversation was, "Pass the salt, please." During dinner no one paid him the slightest attention, chatting away gaily as he sat silently, preoccupied with his food or gazing about without expression as he chewed. Could this be the dynamic political giant we knew?

But!!! Once in his element as leader, business tycoon, politician, Presidential Candidate — WATCH OUT! These were the roles he had studied for, the ones he fit as no one else could because he had made them his. As the "man," he became these parts, and that's what all good leaders do: become what they have to, to get the job done.

On the ride back to my Scottsdale hotel, I played at the game of imagining "Mr. Goldwater of the restaurant" rising to the platform amidst the thunderous applause of the convention, staring down at his notes, fidgeting with his glasses, glancing around the hall and asking directions to the men's room.

I become unreasonably angry with lackadaisical executives whose staggering egos allow them to present themselves as they really are, sort of — in the buff? Disaster! There are damned few men or women who can eliminate the packaging and still be effective as leaders. Or anything else for that matter.

Spare me the executive who tackles meetings unprepared or conferences with too few simple notes or no notes at all. Executive egoists, so satisfied with themselves they even ignore the basics of proper seating, adequate lighting, lecture props and preparation. For championship "I don't give a crap" form, give me the "great ones," who arrive at the same time or slightly after their audience.

Every appearance an executive makes should be considered with the possible exception of going to the toilet, and perhaps that as well. The person running the place should look the part even then.

A real no-brainer is an executive sitting in his office with the door closed. There may be an occasional need for privacy or quiet contemplation, but when you shut the door you remove your presence along with whatever motivation it's supposed to create. With the door shut, your image is now a door, in fact, a closed door, which may be necessary while you change your pants or press your skirt, and then I'm not too sure. Unless absolutely impossible, a boss must stay visible, look good, supply energy — all the things that make a difference. Privacy doesn't make you special, just invisible.

It's important that leaders hold forth a special image, especially for their employees. Being yourself may have a nice ring, but it's questionable whether it will be what your people want or need. As leaders, do we really want to appear as everyone else? Human ... yes, friendly, warm, caring ... yes. Like everyone else ... I think not.

DID YOU SAY PEOPLE SKILLS?

PEOPLE SKILLS — *that without which we lose valuable people and if we're lucky, our attorney along with them.*

Practically every failure or success in life can be traced to People Skills or the lack of them. However, in my eyes, "People Skills" is bad terminology. For one thing, it hints of manipulation, shrewdness and skullduggery, which is probably as far from the truth as some other opinions I've had. The above very strong quote infers, however, that if you're working with people you damned well better be skillful at it. This being the case, it follows that executives lacking the talent are worthless. At least as executives.

For anyone new to the responsibilities of leadership, it will soon be apparent that the most important step in their career when they transit from the security of their own production to dependency on the production of others. From then on, their success will depend on the extent of their People Skills.

Every book on management, salesmanship or leadership concerns itself in one way or another with People Skills, which in its simplest form is the ability, regardless of circumstances, to work amicably with others; to make all people situations fruitful. In this sense, these skills are totally responsible for the quality and longevity of marketplace relationships.

All associates fall into two categories: those I enjoy working with and those I don't. Surprisingly, the returns from the relationship doesn't determine the issue. Good relationships are those to which both parties equally contribute their personality, humor, affability, caring, etc., features that enhance the chances for success. These are the relationships hat are worth having.

Regardless of these needed values, the roots of successful relationships will almost always depend on an ability to "get along," a circumstance calling for compromise, adjustment and understanding.

Being well liked indicates the presence of People Skills, providing that being well liked is just part of the picture and not the picture. To lead efficiently and be well liked is the ultimate in People skills; the ability to fulfill your own role without interfering with the role of others' true artistry.

Acquiring this important form of "know-how'" starts with realizing that the basic skills are there; all that needs doing is to identify them. People Skills are old hat, and as you already know what we're talking about, what remains is sorting out the tools and going to work.

However, should you still doubt this special pocket of knowledge, look around you, the answers are all there … people. Mike Lawless, a dear friend and very smart, thought of businesses as HUMAN RELATIONS LABORATORIES, and right he was. In every office situation one is exposed to an endless variety of homo-sapiens; observing them as they adjust to one another and develop into a bunch of happy campers is a People Skill revelation!

To succeed you must want to learn. Books help but in the end, skill with people requires desire, determination and practice. "Getting along" under any circumstance, adjusting to people and becoming the leader you want to be, well … good luck. You may not make it all the way, but even half way nets you a kiss on both cheeks.

THE DEPRESSED ART OF CHEWING ASS

IT'S A SAD SET of circumstances, but the short supply of applicants in today's marketplace has eroded "boss" confidence and all but put an end to staff reprimands. What we have now is a nightmare of frustration for any employer with a normal appetite for ass-chewing. "Vengeance shall be mine, sayeth the Lord," has lost any real significance, at least as it may apply to employee relations.

It didn't happen overnight, in fact, it took years for "chewing" expertise to reach its present state, one in which there is little to take pride. For various reasons, positions have reversed themselves; employees who couldn't do enough to please me now do me a favor by showing up for work. Should they arrive on time and fully clothed, I place grapes and other offerings in a small shrine I keep hidden in my office. Perhaps I should do more?

Quite sadly, the switch from ass chewers to ass kissers has taken the fun out of owning a business. Sometimes I don't even feel like going to work.

As compensation, my sense of retribution has sharpened; "pay-back" scenarios are more carefully thought out and my impromptu lightning strikes are becoming legend. For example, I contribute generously to a profit sharing plan, thus creating a false sense of security that will fall apart and devastate them when the market crashes. Then there's my twenty-five-cent fine for chewing gum ... catch them every time, a little thing I learned from Captain Queeg and great fun.

Financial accountability and good cash flow have put an end to motivation ruses such as: "Sure hope there's enough money to pay you this week," the sort of thing that used to get the week off to a good start. Right now I'm planning an across-the-board raise which should keep them off balance for awhile. Actually, the raise is pay-back against staff that quit before I could fire them. When they hear about the raise, they'll just die.

> ***My object all sublime ... I shall achieve in time ... Let the punishment fit the crime.***
> ... *W.S. Gilber ... .The Mikado*

In the good old days when workers were paid two and three dollars an hour and sometimes not even that, there was a sense of order about things. Now we worry about health care and poverty levels, and it hasn't helped a bit, they still demand more training and better supervision and are leaning suspiciously toward things like group dynamics where they can appear to be interested in the company future. Pretty slick.

Too, when staff members have been with you too long, they start taking an unsolicited proprietary interest in the business — doing things before you tell them to, or coming to work early — "getting things prepared for the day," they say, I'll bet they are.

Then there's the smart Alecs. This morning I asked a new employee why he was in at ten-thirty when he wasn't due until twelve. His reply, with a staged forlorn look, "I have no life." Very funny, very funny. Robbed of my usual sharp retorts, all I got out of the exchange was a good laugh, which I thoroughly resented.

And they're clever, calling in if they're going to be even ten minutes late, bringing doctors' slips when they're absent only a day, taking personal time to visit sick clients, and to a man, sending Christmas and birthday cards. Talk about phoney! Under the guise of "career," they improve every day, just like the higher pay and bonuses have nothing to do with it. Actually, they'll do anything to upset you.

I can take almost anything, but seeing the end of asschewing is tragic. What good is being a boss if you can't scream at someone for no reason. I've got to do something, I'm starting to feel good about them.

The act of "chewing ass," according to Peter Drucker, who wouldn't use the term if it guaranteed him a best seller, is a form of discipline, the goal of which is "control," a synonym for "direction." One Plane Geometry axiom says, "Things equal to the same thing are equal to each other," so "chewing" must be a form of "Direction! So, all the time I chomped away, like some mad green-eyed monster, I was only offering directions. Makes sense, but it wasn't what I intended.

It seems then, that ass chewing as a solution to employee problems no longer plays a role in the scheme of things. Experts declare that reasoning is the answer, which for unreasonable leadership is over the cusp. For management willing to use their heads instead of their authority, it should be an interesting experience. In outlawing verbal attacks on personnel, we exchange "might for right," which makes it important to know what we're talking about.

In today's business world, winning the "I lead, you follow" game can no longer be accomplished with fear; intimidation, temper tantrums and ass chewing are fading luxuries which may, if we're not careful, extend our life expectancy.

Distrust anyone in whom the impulse to punish is too powerful.   ... *Friederick Nietzsche*

LONESOME? HAVE A MEETING

ONE AWESOME POWER of management is the ability to call a meeting any time they feel like it. Staff may be busting their buns trying to keep the company in business, but if the boss wants a meeting, regardless how frivolous, they "come a running." In view of some meetings I've attended, that they respond at all defines the word "authority."

However, good meetings are fun and give staff an opportunity to join the party. If a shortage of enthusiasm for meetings exists, chances are they haven't been too swift in the past. A little more preparation perhaps ... better material I wonder ... a few laughs maybe ... discontinuing, do you think?

The average work day being autocratic in nature, it offers minimal bi-lateral communication. All the more reasons for gatherings offering latitude for company commercials and relief from starched routines. Assuming, of course, that they're good ones. Bad meetings are like bad movies, except no one can leave. They are also counter-productive.

Meetings must be democratic in nature, opinions should be sought, lines of communication established, and the meaning of "teamwork" exploited strongly. Meetings should open communications for all, regardless of rank. In good meetings, the pecking order is established and the hierarchy becomes apparent. In meetings, future plans materialize and work takes on meaning. Most important: in meetings the boss has an opportunity to sell what needs selling the most ... himself.

The formula is simple:

KEEP IT INTERESTING, KEEP IT EXCITING, AND KEEP IT SHORT!

Keep it interesting: Staff meetings should focus on things that concern staff. If this isn't the case, then there are methods of involvement that will create the interest you need. To promote involvement, solicit opinions, ask for suggestions, all of which gives them a voice in the decision-making and creates interest. To encourage longevity, it is important staff be included in your plans.

Unfortunately, vital subjects and their details make for boring meetings. However, they can be tempered somewhat by avoiding lecturing. There's nothing the matter with lectures, but if it's going to be a lecture, then call the damned thing a lecture, not a meeting, "Today, I have a lecture 'for you' or 'on you,' or is it 'at you,' not a meeting with you." Expecting one and getting the other makes for negative results.

To keep meetings exciting: DO SOMETHING PHYSICAL! Physical action motivates and comes in many simple forms. Action focuses audience attention: oral testing, the use of props or a blackboard, impromptu demonstrations, imaginative simulations, reading aloud from manuals, standing on your head, dropping your pants, whatever.

Moving about or fidgeting is not what were' talking about and is nerve-racking for the audience. Unless it has a purpose, speaking from a sitting position is ludicrous. When seated you become part of the audience, so who's holding the meeting? You may not be a great speaker, but if you're standing, at least you look the part. This impression may change as soon as you open your mouth, but that's something else.

For exciting meetings, GET EXCITED YOURSELF! Excitement, like the measles, is contagious, but someone has to get infected first, and I guess that's you. Despite the youth of today's management, there's a prevailing geriatric mood, a fear someone may think they're alive. These are the "Tell it," not "sell it" speakers, who act like nothing matters ... ho hum. Well, something does matter, like the audience and acting like they matter will get their attention. Watch a minister sell God to his congregation; like crazy stories, threats, promises, heaven, hell and damnation, and considering what an easy sell God is, one has to admire their intensity.

Laughter is a great audience stimulant. Avoid coming off light-headed, but don't be afraid to laugh and have fun. Few of us are natural comics, so be careful; ad libbing is something even professionals avoid. If people have fun at your meetings, they'll want more of them. Laughing and learning is a bonding experience. If you enjoy a meeting, you feel you've learned something whether you have or not. People are more open and responsive when they're relaxed and having fun.

Keep it short: By organizing your material, you can keep it short and still accomplish everything you want and more. It isn't that you want the meeting to BE short, you want it to SEEM short, which it will if it's fun. Meetings should be exciting and alive unless in honor of the recent dead, and then more so.

Meetings offer management opportunities to shine, to exercise their real authority ... INFLUENCE! Plan well, know what you want to accomplish, present the material intelligently and enjoy! They can be the highlight of the day for staff or what they dread the most. It will help your attitude and effort to remember that they work to make money, and they'd be making some if they weren't sitting in your meeting. So make the damned thing worthwhile so they don't resent being there.

ON MY SIGNAL ... "BONZAI!"

WOULD THAT IT WERE that simple, just yell "CHARGE," and employees go tearing into their projects screaming, "GERONIMO!" Right? I don't think so.

In the first place, when I yell "charge," not everyone realizes it's me. They may have worked for me for years, but I can tell by their expressions that they haven't quite placed me. Either that or they're more indifferent to me than I thought. Like most bosses, I never really know what staff is thinking about, and it's a cinch they're not going to tell me. If anyone has solved this, I'm listening.

After fifty years of various motivational failings, I decided to take a whack at "why" they exist. Here then are my opinions as to why some executives have the power to motivate and others don't. For one thing, those who can have probably read a book on motivation, exposing a lack of creative ability, but proving they can read.

There's also the chance there are staffs made up of toadies with a toadies crippling compulsion to please. These come about because of radical management ideas: that staff should earn above the poverty level, have better working conditions, paid vacations, sick pay, etc. Some becoming so depraved they provide profit sharing, health insurance, annual cost of living raises and child care allowances. Pretty bad.

If by chance management earns staff respect, then let it

be on their own heads. A staff that respects the boss probably respects his decisions as well, and that shoots everything to hell. What the poor sod has done is convince staff he can be trusted! Can you imagine! A boss you can trust! Makes you want to throw up.

The worst of these are those who make staff accomplishments appear worthwhile. What on earth for? Why should it be necessary to compliment work they're being paid to do? Seems to me a man should have something better to do with his time. And they actually charge!

Motivation is not some mystic power that moves people against their will. Motivation is an enthusiasm for accomplishment born from shared ideas. When everyone is working toward the same goal, when all co-dependents share the same struggle, who's motivating who? What they're sharing is a state of mind.

Synonyms for Motivation: To move, to activate, to incite, to provoke, to turn on, to SET ON FIRE, to instigate, to start, to move, to propel, to drive, to force, to railroad, to spur, to prod, to egg on, to urge, to coddle, to wheedle, to cajole, to manipulate, to influence, to persuade ... to bring around to see your way.

If you haven't been too motivating in the past, perhaps you weren't aware of the above options. Once having studied this list of available ways and means, there's little reason not to do a better job of it, and no mention was made of my favorite, "to threaten!"

Webster on Motivation: TO PROVIDE WITH OR AFFECT A MOTIVE!!!

That the word MOTIVATION is built on the word MOTIVE has never occurred to me. To motivate, one provides motives! Magnificent!!!

BLUE SKIES OR THE BLUES — IT'S YOUR CALL

THE WORDS Blue Sky are interesting and can mean many things. As the words of a song, "There'll Be Blue Skies From Now On," they hold forth promise and happiness. Used to describe phony stock deals, they stand for exaggeration and false promises. When working with staff, Blue Skies are their future, that intangible "sometime" just out of reach, a brightening, a way, a new life, money, position, control, freedom and an easing of concerns. All elusive to the average worker.

If, according to Drucker (and I humbly concur), the main responsibility of a business is to stay in business, then keeping staff with you long enough to become experienced and smart enough to do the job is a prime priority.

Because staff capabilities are coincidental with their experience, holding onto them until they have a little is a must. Not too easy in view of the restlessness of youth. Without anything better to look forward to, they soon get a temporary look in their eyes. In the absence of a future change or improvement, their disappearance is just a matter of time, and that, my friend, is the end of both your ball games.

Generally speaking, staff shows little interest in job promotions or growth, seemingly content to earn enough money to support their lifestyle, whatever it may be. I strongly believe this is a misconception and that it will be the "content" ones who will leave you first. They may not speak of it on the job, but in their down time, want ads are their favorite reading.

How long it takes a sub-conscious "rut" to affect seemingly content employees is hard to say; the variables are many. You can bet the farm, however, that if such a rut exists, it's just a matter of time. "Burn-out," probably the most hackneyed of all employee justifications for quitting, suggests they've worked so hard for so long, they have nothing more to give — sheer crap. The truth is they're bored. What was once an exciting job has become dull!

So, one sunny day when nothing could possibly go wrong, your most enthusiastic and industrious employee, the one you never had to waste a second worrying about, Mr. Dependable, knocks on your door, extols eternal gratitude for everything you've done for him and quits. Sometimes with no more notice than the time it takes to clean out his locker. Only slaughterhouse boredom or an incredible job offer could spike a move like that! In a blink a valuable staff member has passed from a "company" man into the dimension, known affably as a "stick your company" man. The problem ... no "Blue Skies."

It may be difficult to understand, but employees aren't aware that it's happening to them. One minute they're enjoying their job, then suddenly there's the feeling they're not getting anywhere, and the only thing that makes sense is a change and that means quitting. With even a smidgen of "Blue Skies," it may have been avoided.

In one of her seminars on personnel, a brilliant lecturer, Molly Witker, asked: "If you were waiting for a bus and it came along without the destination on the monitor at the front, would you get on?" Of course not, you'd want to know where it was going first. That the same principle applies to staff getting into a new situation isn't surprising. They have to know where they're going before they get on.

Creating "futures" is a leadership responsibility. Employees must feel they have a definitive role in the future of the business. If opportunities for promotion are few, then delegate them responsibilities as a substitute. Money may feed us, but a sense of getting somewhere is food for the soul.

Itemize the details of your day, then carefully select duties you feel they can perform and simply "hand them over." By enlarging their area of responsibility, you open the door to the future. Delegating is also an important safety valve for executives long on ideas and short on time. Besides giving them breathing space, it may save an employee.

The two main laws governing delegating are: 1. Delegate, don't abdicate! If you unload duties but don't supervise and display interest, the unloadee soon realizes that all you've done is given him a pat on the head, and that all you did was get him off your back. With that, the project is blown

Law No. 2: Work that isn't paid for is "favors," and doing "favors" for you isn't what we had in mind when we spoke of delegating. For services rendered, an employee should get paid. The days of displaying a good attitude by working overtime without pay went out with the dinosaurs. Besides, money lends dignity to work; work without money is degrading.

Through intelligent delegating, almost any position within the company can be expanded endlessly. Delegating is one solution to the problem; it can also take the form of developing assistants for: functions, meetings, training, customer services, personnel work, buddy teams, etc. Work projects can also be effective, i.e., determining departmental efficiency, investigating Guerrilla marketing, advertising, sales promotions, customer satisfaction polls, etc., etc., etc.

Committees. Various committee assignments have kept Congressmen, Senators and Vice Presidents in valuable government positions long after they might have been attracted to more lucrative fields. They can do the same for you, but nothing comes without its price, and committees are no exception. The price is time, your time, although I can't think of anything better you could do with it. The business health of employees paves your future or the absence of one. By enlarging employee opportunities, you enlarge your own.

With programs such as these, employees soon acquire a different perception of their position, how it relates to the company and their future in it.

Once we understand that, for an employee, growth doesn't necessarily mean more income. Take-home pay may be all-important, but no more than future, position and self-respect. Money itself is seldom enough to satisfy anyone's long range needs. Job satisfaction lies in a belief in the future. With it, work becomes worth doing. Without "Blue Sky," the greatest job in the world becomes mundane. With nothing to look forward to, there's little worth working for.

They say about parenting that, "If you do everything perfectly, chances are the child will thrive in spite of you." After everything we've discussed, you may still lose the employee, but at least it won't have been your fault. If you've done your part and they still leave, to hell with them.

In the best seller, "What Makes Sammy Run?" asked how he likes his job, Sammy replies, "I like it fine this year. If I still have it next year, it stinks."

A great book. I never liked the character of "Sammy," but he made sense.

PERKS, PRIVILEGES AND PROTOCOL

CORPORATE PRIVILEGES of rank, snidely referred to as the "keys to the executive toilet," are usually the property of high-paid executives with a secretary smarter than themselves. They also have an office with a window that opens, a company car and an expense account for things they could never afford otherwise. Great conversation pieces in the muffled flushing of posh company rest-rooms, and the not-so-muffled toilets of the Internal Revenue Service.

Although perks are rewards of a kind, they seldom have anything to do with performance. These "extras" are mysteriously linked to certain positions and become the property of whoever happens to be in them. Like everything else, perks are not without a price. Protocol says that anyone rising above the crowd who tries to remain as part of that crowd will not be smiled upon. Becoming an executive means you are no longer like the others, so you damned well better not act like you are!

For example, lunching with whom you please certainly seems harmless enough, and there's little question your secretary or that cute receptionist would be fun. However, unless you intend to promote, fire or marry them, the date is verboten. In either case, lunch isn't deductible.

In the aftermath of a fun lunch with the boss, secretaries, receptionists, or for that matter, any employee, will probably view future dealing with the boss through the misty veil of the vin rouge they enjoyed together. And when other employees see you laughing together intimately, they will suspect instantly ... instantly that you're laughing about them. After all, whatever else in the world could you be laughing at? All in all, lunches with employees is a lousy idea.

History also reflects that most of us are incapable of much professionalism once we've breached the master-slave syndrome. Too bad, when you think about it.

One of the great sacrifices one makes when dwelling in the land of corporate perks is the privilege, when in a fit, to tell an employee to piss off! Or for that matter, the right to throw a fit at all. Inhuman! During the golden years management ruled with fear, and if the situation called for it, a threat of bodily harm. Perhaps in bad taste, but it didn't seem so at the time. No more! A successful executive, (I'm starting to dislike the word more every day) must, because of legal frailties, find other corporate releases for their passions.

Take behavior patterns. The exec with a bottle of Jim Beam on his desk was once considered "friendly." Today he'd be considered a drunk. Forget the bottle on the desk, a cocktail at lunch can get you the same reputation. Too, if your car's too big, your house too posh, your wife too blonde, or you look like you have nothing to worry about, you'll suffer a severe drop in credibility. Employees want you to be "the man," but on their terms, which means not being too content or well off.

As an executive, what people see you do isn't as important as what they think you do. So, play it safe; if you take your secretary to lunch, take everyone, and if you have to do that, why bother? More than anything, you must be perceived as "trustworthy." If not, you are lost, and no one trusts a man who chases his secretary. Whether you catch him/her or not isn't the point, to workers it's an abuse of power, and for the secretary, a possible juicy harassment suit.

Then we have favoritism! A word to die for! The boss

who falls prey to this temptation has literally "had it!" Once guilty of favoritism, you can forget about motivation. Play favorites, and you'll not only be have to function without motivation, you won't be able to spell it.

Wouldn't it be great if you could get away with it. There they stand, your favorite staff member, laughs at your jokes, takes notes whenever you say anything, listens closely when you belch, is always on time, always productive and has great legs (Choose your own gender). And what do you do: compliment them openly, smile at them differently, laugh loudly at their jokes, brazenly compare their work to others, and by doing so, DESTROY THEM! It's just a matter of time before they'll be doing fast food.

The word is "EQUALITY" or "SAMENESS!!!" Spread the smiles, laugh at everyone's jokes and compliment in groups. You won't have any fun, but it works.

The position of "Executive" is something we may have earned and are entitled to, but we still have to live with it. Strike the two "F's," *favoritism and fraternizing,* from your consciousness, at least as they regard staff ... life will be a lot simpler and probably more worthwhile.

WHATCHA THINK?

BARNES AND NOBLE, bookseller to the world, stock thousands of books and every year add thousands of new issues to their already bulging shelves. Public libraries pick up where they leave off with millions of volumes, a large portion of which are already out of print. The national archives contains millions of volumes not included by either book stores or libraries, and throughout the world books fill nooks and crannies in every home, office, library and museum. The numbers of books that have been written, like computations involving the cosmos, is beyond comprehension. So, books must sell. However, Oscar Levant says as only Levant could:

> *I've given up reading books. I find it takes my mind off myself.*

It bothers me then that so few of us spend time putting "pen to paper." Even letter writing, once a social grace, has reduced itself to fax messages. Can you remember the last time you wrote a letter other than a product complaint or a note to the maid?

The purpose of this chapter is to encourage writing on a larger scale. Like teen-age tea parties with all the girls on one side of the room and the boys on the other, the adult world seems to have placed writers on one side of the paper, and readers on the other; the idea being that writers read but readers seldom write. Our friends from the British slums would call this a "bloomin' shame." It's also a blooming loss.

You may ask," What does writing have to do with leadership?" The answer is nothing except that writing has to do with "thinking," and that ... has to do with leadership. I doubt Socrates concerned himself about what publishing company would pick up his options, or if Ben Franklin watched for his monthly royalty checks. Yet they wrote endlessly because in writing they found answers, not because they were writing, but because they were thinking. Writing does that.

The same opportunity is there for everyone. Unlike these great men, what happens to civilization isn't our first priority; however, training staff is, and as developing leadership qualities is what we're discussing, it's certainly apropos. Instead, we think, "We'll just buy another book and it will tell us what to do," and it will, and, we'll forget it in the same time span it took us to forget all the other stuff we've read. In finding our own direction, finding self-prescribed answers, the results are ours forever.

> ***We all want to be smart. I've never met anyone who wanted to be stupid. We all want answers, but too few are willing to sit down and find them.***

Thinking through to conclusions isn't easy, thoughts are elusive, in your head one minute and gone the next. For instance, when writing music, the theme you just composed, that haunting melody that will live forever! Well, whatever it was doesn't stay with you long enough to go get coffee. So, don't lose it, PUT IT ON PAPER. By writing it down, you've staked your claim, it's yours to have and covet forever.

Memos to yourself may not be an art form, but they're the beginning of one. From memos come developed thought, inspirations for new ideas, procedures, training. A memo about something you've seen in passing can produce a new procedure or change one already in use, a training program, a manual, better service, improved income.

One manager, a great San Francisco gal, kept memo pads everywhere she might pause in the course of a day or night; on her nightstand, in her office, in her car, in the bathroom, the kitchen. Her mind, like yours, was working constantly, the difference was, she didn't trust it to hold onto things, so she jotted down memos — about everything. From the notes she developed, thoughts and thoughts became action. Ideas hit and run; thought is the seed but watering and growing makes the thoughts pay off, and this is what writing accomplishes!

What happens when you simply sit and think, when you shut out the world and let your mind tip-toe through the daisies? For me — nothing. Sitting and thinking, like working out in a gym, is boring, I find it difficult to concentrate and nothing happens. But when I write, I can stand on my head blindfolded with earmuffs and be productive. The image of myself as a writer is stimulating, whereas meditation, in any form, leaves me blah. However, that's me; for you, it might work, but if it does, then write it down or you'll forget it.

Don't misunderstand, writing doesn't come easy, and when it does come, a lot of crap comes with it. The crap, however, is yours, all yours, and with a little work, who knows? Writing develops ideas that can be preserved until you have the time to consider whether you really want them, will keep them, develop them or discard them. Talented speakers are few, but through writing anyone can be heard.

Writing takes time because thinking takes time. Once you've decided to think for yourself, there are no quick fixes. Critiquing someone else's thoughts may be a form of thinking, but it's not creative; it's latch-on, a dependent action.

> ***Once you've cultivated the ability to develop your own ideas, then your opinions concerning the ideas of others, become valid.***

For executives in today's marketplace, creative opportunities are endless: meetings, projects, directives, procedures, types of presentations, business manuals, ad writing, sales scripts, press releases, staff lectures, etc., etc., etc.

Should writing ever become part of your psyche, you'll be hooked forever; there's something totally fascinating about filling page after page with your thoughts, and nothing is more "you" than what you put on paper.

ALTRUISTIC ... WHO, ME?

DISCOVERING I PLAY the piano, people, without considering the consequences, start acting like their lives will never be the same until they hear me play. Whether they're buttering me or not is unimportant, this is the way they are programmed. Perhaps they really want to hear me play, but I'm inclined to think part of it is to make me feel good, and other than giving people money, there's nothing nicer you can do for them and it's cheaper.

Absorbed with our own emotions or what's going to happen to us next, doing for others becomes secondary. Not including Mother's Day, or some forced gurgling over a newborn who looks like Toni Canzonerri after a fight, we do precious little to make people feel good. Certainly not enough.

The acts of fibbing, stretching the truth, praising the not-so-praiseworthy and putting things on deposit for the purpose of improving relationships, are known in some circles as diplomacy, which according to Webster means: "The skill of dealing with people." Making others feel good about themselves is one of these skills.

I've had the good fortune to have been associated with one of these born diplomats for forty years, and I'll tell you now that the positive effect has made the largest single difference in my business life. To my knowledge this unique human has never passed up an opportunity to make people feel good about themselves. That she also happens to be the ultimate person in her field doesn't hurt.

Knowing her is a lesson in selflessness, the real kind, not the "I hope this works for me" kind.

Do I emulate her? Of course not! I'm me, not her, and I wouldn't change dispositions if I could. I might be better off, but it wouldn't be me. When she says something nice, she means it, or does she? What's the difference, nice is nice.

Mike Lawless, a fine leader and human being I was fortunate to call friend, claimed that the prime characteristics of good leadership is "selflessness," which I interpret as being altruistic and dedicated to the interest of others rather than, or as well as your own.

"Very difficult!" you say, and, you're right. I know of few people I think of as selfless. So, leadership is easy? You know a big bunch of great "leaders" maybe? Why would leadership be undemanding and the results so rewarding? What great dish is easy to prepare? The recipe for leadership is as complicated and demanding as putting together a great meal. If being "selfless" is one of the ingredients, then, regardless of the degree of difficulty, hadn't we better look into it?

Getting a "10" for an Olympic dive will depend on two things: execution and degree of difficulty. Leadership should be regarded the same. If it comes easy, then chances are you're not executing right, or haven't assumed the real problems, the ones that develop that degree of difficulty. Introducing "selflessness" into your personal repertoire can go a long way to earn a "10" and maybe an "11."

Being selfless can make you feel even better about yourself than playing the piano, and it's only half as hard. I think.

AN INCREDIBLY CREDIBLE PERSON

B RINGING ST. PETER or Mahatma Ghandi into our treatise on "leadership" may seem a little much, but class is class and a few halos or white muslin sheets can't hurt. The point: because of their deeds and personal behavior, people believed them and in them. What they became in their lifetimes was "incredibly credible," people beyond reproach. Considering their fate, however, playing copycat may be something we want to think twice about. Something today's politicians have little to be concerned about.

Amongst other things, there's an enormous satisfaction in being believed and, strangely enough, it isn't the accuracy of your vision or the success of your investments that makes this happen. What makes a person believable is the honesty and spirit of what they say and the conviction with which they say it. Becoming an "incredibly credible" person has little to do with being right, but then again, how often do we listen to losers?

Meaning what you say and thinking things through before you say them is what credibility is all about. Being known as "incredibly credible" ain't easy. For this kind of "rep," "truthfulness" is more important than accuracy or success. People speaking from the heart are often as wrong as they're right, but if it's from the heart, people are inclined to overlook your being wrong. What credibility has to do with it is saying what you believe without fudging. Once caught with foot in mouth or speaking with forked tongue, in all probability you've killed your chances for the title of "incredibly credible" forever!

Too, the importance or unimportance of your lie has nothing to do with it. Regardless how eentzy-weentzy it may seem to you, they'll never let you off the hook. Don't depend on some sweet soul saying, "What's the difference, it wasn't important," or ... "Think of all the good things he's done." Forget it. Give them a little balloon and they'll turn it into the Graf Zepplin. The best you may get is "I wonder why he/she — said/did that, that's not like him/her." But they'll never forget it; you gave them a gift and they're not about to return it.

You earn your credibility wings from the inside out, and you can't fake it. Either you're a credible person or you're not, and it doesn't come in bunches, like — today you're credible, tomorrow you're not. Can people lacking credibility be successful? YASSUH! Can they become great leaders — I don't think so.

> ***Speak the truth, but leave immediately after.***
> *... Slovenium proverb.*

Credibility isn't about what you are, it's about who you are. Take a look at today's politicians, the leaders of the country, that's what they are, but the "who" tells us they are incapable of the truth unless it's self-serving. These apparently incorrigible people are only where they are because we needed someone to lead and there were incredibly few options. We line them up, then vote for the phoney with the most appeal.

Qualifying for credibility laurels is tough because the margin for error is non-existent:

How honest must you be?	100%
How accurate must you be?	Unimportant as long as you're honest
How right must you be?	Refer to accuracy

No one expects perfection, but they do expect leaders to make a run at it. An essential part of it is their credibility, how much stock others can put in what they say. It avails nothing to plan great agendas, hold motivating meetings or carry the banner forward if no one's following or listening, and no one is listening unless they believe.

If the job is done right, a boss does more than fill a chair at the end of the boardroom table; he/she fulfills the employees' and the company's need for credible leadership. Of all the distinctions available to management, being believable is probably the toughest, the most valuable and the most enduring.

When you stretch the truth, watch out for the snap back. ... *Bill Copeland*

INVOLVEMENT — THE FINAL SOLUTION

SOME BRIGHT PERSON once said, "Enthusiasm for something comes with the doing of it," which sounds like putting the cart before horse or whatever it is you pull a cart with these days.

Then my pinpoint reasoning takes over and I realize he was right. Obviously, enthusiasm stemming from participation will not only be more efficient, it will last longer. Too, the principle of "Enthusiasm through involvement" will take care of most of your problems because it applies equally well to anything: sales, religion, romance, sports. We face the problem of getting people involved every day of our business life. However, once you can get them into the act, the rest is dancing.

Consider sales ... of anything. Be it product or service, a sale usually relies on a demonstration of some sort, and if the prospect is involved, so much the better. Watching a vacuum salesman suck your cat up along with the dirt doesn't hold the emotional wallop of sucking the little critter up yourself.

The salesman who convinces you to vacuum your house so he can sell you a new machine is the one I want to hire. If the machine is this good, it could probably get rid of visiting relatives as well.

After talking you into vacuuming the house for him, a

good vacuum salesman points out the emotional benefits of his super-sucker: **1.** How easy it was to operate and always will be. **2.** How keeping the work easy will keep you young. **3.** How good your house smells compared to the way it smelled before. **4.** How your friends will comment about your nice smelling house and how young you look. **5.** How this will give you time for all the things you've always wanted to do, like vacuuming your friends' houses.

Demonstrating how something works may be entertaining but physically involving the prospect as you point out the lasting emotional benefits, sells!!. And, that's the point, isn't it?

Once a salesman involves the prospect, the rest is easy. "HERE Y'AH, get your complimentary this and that right here! Try a free trial 'this,' or a free ride on a very fast 'that' — stretch yourself out on that there new springless bed — jump into the new waterless swimming pool — peddle this wheel-less bike or take your true love for a free dinner at "Joe's herbal diner," you'll love it! Anything to get you involved because they know !!! INVOLVEMENT SELLS!

Your attorney, bless him, convinces you that you have a case you can't lose, when in truth, he couldn't win it with Clarence Darrow sitting on his lap. He knows, however, that once you're involved, you're dead, there's no way out. And so it goes — get people involved in your agenda, whatever it may be, and your chances for success are excellent.

Education is a test-tube example of the power of involvement. Young people pay through the nose for an education that they haven't a clue what to do with. They spend years in classrooms studying subjects they can't relate to for a certificate they can hardly read, to hang on an office wall they haven't got. In the end the jobs they thought they were training for are either taken or obsolete. McDonald's, here we come.

To succeed in business requires the ability to involve people in your plans and train your employees to do likewise. Involvement does away with the need for beau coup talk, whether you're selling employees on ideas or prospects on product. Involvement is effective; it overcomes lassitude and indifference through involvement.

> ***More good things in life are lost by indifference than by active hostility.***   *... Robert Menzies*

SOME GAME PLAN — DON'T LOSE!

VINCE LOMBARDI, famed coach of the Greenbay Packers, made a statement to the world on national television that:

> ***"Winning wasn't the best thing, it was the only thing."***

With those words he had every poor bastard who had never beaten anyone in their life at anything hating his guts. However, if he was right and winning is the "only" thing, then maybe we should learn the secret of how to become a winner, which I think begins with your mindset at the start of whatever the game may be.

> ***Aggressively positive:*** *"I'm going to bust this baby wide*
> ***Intelligent and careful,*** *"This looks interesting, I'll probably do quite well."*
> ***Worst case scenario:*** *"It will be tough, I hope I make it."*

Like it or not, how you think will articulate every move you make and the force with which you make it.

A man said to a canary he was holding, "Your fate is in my hands," and he was right. It didn't matter how much chirping the canary did or how he struggled, his fate depended on someone else's intentions. Unlike that bird, your fate isn't in anyone's hands, maybe not even your own. Most likely it's in your head, the way that you think. So, a little head work, please ... a Game Plan maybe?

> ***Game plans:*** *Complicated outlines of plays and strategies coaches are fond of losing with.*

As game plans represent a coach's thinking, they protect whatever the results are at all costs: "The plan was great, we just executed badly." Or, "Nothing the matter with the game plan, we just didn't have the right personnel" — like someone changed teams on them when they weren't looking. The very purpose of a Game Plan is to overcome problems caused by inadequate personnel, the absence of expert execution or other shortages that may occur.

Maybe Game Plans don't work all of the time, but the basic concept, "Be Prepared," did well for the Boy Scouts, and if it was good enough for Davey Crockett and Buffalo Bill, it's good enough for me.

The cute part about Game Plans is their adaptability to the size of the project. Almost everything you attempt in life has the same basic parts, but in different forms and sizes. That being the case, the format of any Game Plan will be much the same regardless what the goals may be: Preparation, training, execution, policing. The best of Game Plans, however, assure you nothing, except that you'll cover all the bases.

> **Achievement is the death of endeavor and the birth of disgust.**
> *... Ambrose Pierce "The Devil's Dictionary"*

His point is well made; Game Plans make sure you'll get there, not that you'll like it when you arrive. The purpose of a properly constructed Game Plan is to get you to your goal in less time and with less effort than you would have experienced without one. If it doesn't do that, then you've wasted your time. However, if you're anything like me, the Plan becomes the project, and before you know it, you're so absorbed in the plan, you forget what the dammed thing was about.

Regardless of the project, your problems will almost always be the same: People and money. It may seem there are other things, but with the right people and enough money, you can make anything work. Without them, your skin is in danger. Addressing your Game Plans in this frame of mind may preserve your sanity — keep your team happy and bring success within reach.

"L" STANDS FOR LOYALTY, LOVE AND LEPROSY

THE QUESTIONABLE EXISTENCE of loyalty in people gives me the whim-whams. Animals are different, loyalty in animals is easy to read: dogs are loyal to a fault, a disloyal pig wouldn't surprise anyone, and don't look for loyalty in cats who, like women, are independent, unpredictable and un-dog like. Did I just lose my female readership?

"Leadership," according to experts, involves the cultivation of loyalty, both in ourselves and those around us. Unfortunately, experts have a propensity for telling us "what to do," but not "how to do it." Considering the difficulty factor involving anything to do with loyalty, this is too bad.

Whether we really want a staff saturated with "Loyalty" is questionable. It may be a precious commodity, but it's loaded with double-edged responsibilities. With a faithful dog, you can read a book or watch television while you pat his loyal head, but you can't do faithful people that way; it doesn't work. Faithful people demand attention.

In fifty years as an employer, I've never felt over-burdened with loyal staff. Either this is the way things are, or perhaps I haven't deserved them. Then again, there's a chance I wouldn't recognize loyalty if I was eating it. What should I be looking for? How do I tell a loyal employee from the garden variety.

Realizing that faithfulness and loyalty are interchangeable helps. Loyalty may have a solid sound, while faithfulness comes across sort of wispy. In the final analysis, however, they're the same. Other synonyms may help to further identify loyalty: constant, unwavering, staunch, steadfast, true, steady. Even with these guidelines, identifying "loyal' employees is tricky. You no sooner start bragging on one for being "steadfast and true" when the S.O.B. takes off with your best customers. Others simply quit without notice.

We're also in trouble when we mistake longevity for faithfulness. Some employees stay forever: is it their loyalty or is it that they can't find another job? Try not paying them for a week and watch ten years of paid-up "loyalty" disappear down the tubes.

Another mistake is attempting to buy loyalty as if it were a commodity. Money seldom begets loyalty. Money will buy energy, know-how, discipline, etc., but loyalty, I'm afraid not. Money may be a necessary ingredient to the relationship, but it's not loyalty-building. Staff views money as something that's coming to them. To an employee, money fulfills a contract; they've done their part, and with the money, you've done yours.

Time spent is a different colored horse. Time spent will build loyalty, maybe not all of it you're looking for, but what else is new? Giving unselfishly of yourself as you conscientiously transfer knowledge, share your "smarts" and develop the "Blue Skies," that make the job worthwhile will perform the trick that money, regardless how much or how graciously bestowed, won't do.

I look at money as a "pay-off" for a job well done, or a dismissal of conscience. In either case, giving money doesn't require much in the way of talent, too easy, and seldom carries the message. Also, the more money you have, the less giving it away is appreciated. Of course, people appreciate getting money, they love money, but we're not discussing appreciation, we're discussing loyalty. Give of your time and you've given of yourself, a deed that even the most blasé of employees will be affected by.

If this is true, then executive responsibilities are more complex than we may have originally thought. If loyalty, the desired by-product of leadership, is not on the market, then your work is cut out for you. Between you and the "Loyal Following" we've heard so much about, lies a mess of bonding, training, building relationships, and maybe a lot more involvement than you planned on.

One pleasant loyalty spin-off is affection. Rarely does one feel loyalty towards someone for whom they have no affection. Time spent with people builds affection and love. It's no mere coincidence that we fall in love with someone we see a lot of. No, we learn affection just as we learn other things. However, it doesn't necessarily follow that because we have an affection for someone that we are loyal to them. The divorce ratio proves that.

Like attracts like. Be loyal to your concepts and faithful to those you work with, and before you know it you'll be surrounded with great emotions: Loyalty, faithfulness, affection ... what more could a relationship ask for?

If you like uninspired, dry, obvious quotations, then you'll love this one:

> ***Only the person who has faith in himself, is able to be faithful to others."***
> *... Erich Fromm, "The Art of Loving"*

DELEGATE OR DUMP — WHICH IS IST?

NEITHER TOM SAWYER nor his boss, Mark Twain, was aware that his ruse for getting other people to paint fences for him had earned him a permanent place on the Executive Action All Pro Team. Now accepted as the Hallmark for "suckering," his fence painting game plan paved the way for every gold-bricker that ever conned someone else into doing his work for him. Today we call it: "Delegating."

Delegating is the art of convincing someone they'll be happier doing your work than their own. However, Tom took it to another plateau ... he not only tricked others into painting the fence for him but made them feel good about themselves while they were doing it! Think about it; first he got them to paint his fence, and then hung around to make sure they whistled while they worked. Formidable!

The trick lies in delegating without abdicating.

"Delegating," or if you prefer — "suckering," as opposed to "dumping" — is as different in quality and effect as robbing someone at gunpoint is to picking their pockets. Delegating, expertly performed, builds self-esteem in the delegatee and wins admirers for the delegator, while dumping gets you as disliked as you might ever dream of being.

Some executives think of passing the buck as delegating authority.

For those not privy to the story of Tom and his fence — what Tom did was let it get around that he was going to paint a fence and made it sound so intriguing, everyone wanted to paint it for him, especially Huck Finn, who went green with envy — literally begging for the job. That part was smart, but even smarter was Tom making like he wanted to do it himself more than anything in the world. This kept the suckers in a state, until finally they wound up painting the whole thing. Then, like that wasn't enough, he accused them of cheating him out of his share of painting. Damn!!! Is that good or is that good?

If he had simply gotten people started with the painting and then walked away (dumped), chances are the suckers may have seen through it early on and left, leaving him with a bunch of paint brushes and an unpainted fence. No, sir, as a delegator, Tom was a real "pro!"

Efficient delegating is as important a talent an executive can have, one of the greats. In addition to getting someone to do the work, a good exec wants to see the job done right, so there's a mess of decisions before you start:

First of all, should the work be delegated at all? If it's a primary responsibility of your position, then of course not. Why take the chance? If they do it well, they might wind up with your job.

Secondly, who will the lucky person be? Can't go too high on the roster or they'll laugh at you. Can't go too low or you can't trust them to do it. No, it has to be someone gullible enough to take it and smart enough to do it. Tough.

Thirdly, how to sell it? You can't lie; exaggerating's okay but not lying. How to make it sound exciting without arousing suspicion — if it's so damned much fun, they may ask, how come you're not doing it yourself.

Authority and work must be delegated if an executive is to grow; try to do everything yourself and you'll go nowhere.

Too, proper delegating is like bestowing honors, selectively and with preparation. What nicer compliment is there? But your job has just started — with one arm around the lucky personae shoulder and a tear in your eye:

1. Explain why you need the help, and how much it will mean.
2. Detail the work you want done and train before turning it over.
3. Implement some tracking device, then use it.
4. Confer on a regular basis with your new assistant about the progress.
5. Give recognition and rewards for a job well done.
6. Use target dates and when completed, formerly end the project.

Delegating builds teams, develops assistants, tests your authority, and increases your understanding of how you relate to people, at least it does if it works. If you blow it, act nonchalant, 'cause you're in trouble.

In retrospect, I'm not so sure dumping isn't a better idea, after all. So you make a few enemies, so what?

If you want a job done right, find a busy man and give it to his secretary.

OF COURSE, I LIKE YOU, IT'S JUST THAT —

"LOOK — I'm only human, If I don't like someone, I don't like them. There's nothing I can do about it. If it's an employee, so what — do I have to like him because he works for me? Who said? No, I'm not gonna fire him, it raises the contribution rate. Besides, I know his type — just wants attention — he'll quit anyway.

As an employer, a leader of men, and a credit to the community, why should I be denied the pleasure of letting someone I dislike know about it? It's okay for me to despise one of your employees, but mine I have to like? This is not only discriminatory, but they have lawyers. I accept that there's no place in business for likes or dislikes, but I can't seem to conform. A long time ago I might have, but there were lots of things I could do a long time ago.

I'll never forget one interview with an unhappy employee where I wasted an hour trying to convince him that never looking at him or speaking to him was my way of building character. And ... as he, being the only one I treated this way, was proof that I liked him better then I did the others. I'm not convinced he believed me.

The song, "What's love got to do with it?" makes a great deal of sense. That you like or dislike an employee should have little bearing on your ability to work with them, which unfortunately isn't the case. Actually, it is virtually impossible for me to treat someone well who is distasteful to me. Perhaps that sounds like I'm within my rights, but what do you do when it causes things to go sour? No company can't afford to lose employees because management is inept, but it will.

What to do? For starters, try to decipher your problem, and it is your problem. Why is this particular person a pain in the backside? If it's something he did, the obvious solution is to confront him with it and work it out one way or another. If it's something you've done, then excuse me, please. In either case, the solution lies just below the conversation level.

If your petulance lies in something you've heard, then you should be defrocked. Even if you've verified it, heard both sides of the rumor, yes — rumor, because that's exactly what things you hear are ... rumors. In any case, there's an excellent chance the real problem lies is the person who carried the tale.

Faced with the questionable attitudes of today's youth, there's a vicarious pleasure in facing them with their inadequacies. However, the chink in this particular armor is a need to be fair. When I'm right, I can really wail, but punishing or firing staff wrongly is an executive blunder from which there is no return. Like a wrongful beheading, apologies are redundant.

A good Exec levels the playing field by accepting that their effect on staff is too important for game playing. Being a little wrong is like being a little pregnant. When appraising employees, you're not privileged to see them as good or bad, ratings must apply to performance alone. You may be justified in condemning bad performances, but if influenced by personal dislike, you're in an area you have no right to be.

I think it's an immutable law in business that words are words, explanations are explanations, but only performance is reality.
... *Harold Green CEO Intnl Tel & Tel*

Even when judging performance, certain laws must prevail, if for no other reason than to preserve your position. The difficulties of living with decisions have been the same since the Crucifixion, so when it comes to passing judgment on others, mulling things over isn't a bad idea.

- Have you changed your standard of judgment to fit your mood?
- Are you ignoring mitigating circumstances for personal reasons?
- Would you judge your children the same way?
- Is the decision worth the indelible effect it may have?
- If you dislike the person, is there someone you should confer with?
- When the smoke clears, will your judgment still be justified?
- Does your punishment fit the crime?

Mulling may spoil your fun, but who said leadership was fun? Satisfying yourself at someone else's expense is akin to drinking too much, the hangover, and you can bet there'll be one, is the terrible conclusion that you've been wrong. And, as with every mistake you'll ever make, the memory of it will never go away. Especially if the problem was ego motivated.

> ***I've never made a decision in my life that wasn't one hundred percent selfish.***
> *... John Updike (The Centaur, 1963)*

Take my hand and walk with me while we dream up clever ways to get even with the scamps who supported by youth and the courage of their convictions haven't listened to us and have been perfectly happy. We won't do anything about it, but we can fantasize.

> ***When they say a man is a born executive, they mean his father owns the business.***

THE NEED TO KNOW — KNOW WHAT?

FROM WHAT I'VE SEEN, most of us put in an honest day's work — pay our dues, as they say. Along with those working for us, with us and under us, we spend our waking hours keeping the wolf, whom I have never met, from the door. Days are pretty much the same for everyone; up in the morning, brush what's left of our teeth, carefully distribute our remaining hair and pat something on so we should smell better. Preparation for a day at the races ... work.

The work place: a "people press" into which a mélange of characters, backgrounds, lifestyles, dispositions, personalities and dress codes disappear every morning to re-appear a few minutes later at various work stations. Whatever their individualities, until they go home again they are all employees.

Accepting this as the way things are may work for employees, but for a boss peering through the façade of unpressed suits, runless hose, smiling dentures and blonde hair with dark roots, it's only the beginning. What appears to the human eye as an acceptable employee may, for that day, not be acceptable at all.

This is about taking employee consciousness to a new level in hopes of acquiring longevity records equal at least to those of itinerant grape-pickers. Assuming employees have the same problems as yourself, enjoy the same lifestyle and is as happy as a sandbag is silly. Unless you've failed to notice, the re-possess notice for their five-year-old Hondas differ in tone from the memo that your BMW tune-up is overdue.

> ***Idealism increases in direct proportion to one's distance from the problem.***
> *... John Galsworthy*

Once they arrive on the job, employees are expected to assume the position and deliver regardless of what may be going on in their lives. After all, what could be different — today's bout the same as yesterday, right Clyde? Well, after fifty years of watching and listening, I accept that today is as different from yesterday as this minute is from the next, and that attitudes and intentions carried to the work place can take a one-hundred-eighty-degree swing with an unhappy phone call, a note pushed under the door, a glimpse of one's mortality or a meaningless slight by someone more important to us than they realized.

But is this as it should be? Should personal circumstances be allowed to interfere. After all, this is WORK, and they **are** getting paid, aren't they?

I understand that kind of thinking, and to a point I agree. After all, work has to go on and they are getting paid. This is NOT an unfair attitude, nor is it cruel or uncaring. What can be cruel and uncaring is that the man in charge may be expecting high performance levels without a clue as to whether they are remotely possible under the existing circumstances! What circumstances?

> ***The leader — manager — boss, who functions without knowledge of the circumstances surrounding his employees should have stayed in bed.***

Need we refer to the ostrich who, head in ground, ass in air, can see the world the only way possible from that position. To the ostrich it appears there are no options. That he could pull his head out of the sand never occurs to him. Stupid bird! A good boss may appear to have his head in the sand, but a hidden pair of eyes do the job. A real boss sees all, knows all, understands all — that's what he does for a living.

That we're not ostriches should help. The responsibilities of leaders and motivators become seriously impeded without some knowledge of what's going on in the feathered heads of the tribe he depends on. Maybe there isn't a thing he can do about it, maybe nothing needs doing, maybe the employees would rather he kept his nose out of things, but there is no way in hell he can know if he doesn't find out.

__Ignorance isn't bliss, it's oblivion.__
... Philip Wylie

THE DREAM TEAM

HAVING A TEAM of champions is nice but unimportant as long as your team thinks like champions. Championship attitude is possible in a NFL football team or a group of garbage collectors, providing the man in charge has the stuff. Collecting good people for a team isn't easy, but it's a helluva lot easier than finding a coach with the right stuff. The ratio of coaches to players fired each year is impressive.

Take a look at the NFL or any major league sport. The Bronx Rotorooters has a lousy season, so they fire coach Stupid, which is easier than firing the team. Now they need a coach, so they hire Coach Jerko who is available because he had just been fired by the Frogmen, which has just hired Coach Stupid because they needed a coach.

Teams, like companies, play musical chairs with top people, firing or hiring the same or identical coaches every year or so. What exactly do they think has changed between the firings and the hirings? Is there something beyond the pale?

> *Management and coaches have one thing in common; like a good man ... nowadays they're hard to find.*

What makes good executives rare and valuable is their ability to take a group of very different individuals and mold them into a successful, working unit. How do they do it, what's the secret?

Consider the problem. Teams that are not doing well sometimes have more talent than the teams that are; the problem is seldom personnel. Usually it's a lack of teamwork which deprives the group of its most important asset, group strength. Unable to function as a unit, directly attributable to the man in charge, accomplishing goals of any sort is out of the question.

The truth is, almost every average employee is capable of making the "Dream Team," providing the head coach has coaching qualifications. Assuming we have a coach who qualifies as well as aspires, what will he do to turn this group of ordinary human beings into a Dream Team or at least a Dreamy Team?

1 He makes them feel that what they're doing has meaning, that the end result has a value other than money. There must be a sense of community, a sense that what they do is worthwhile. Money can be the results of your work, but for the long range it cannot be the purpose for which the work is performed.

2. He must imbue the group with that sense of competition mandatory to the success of any group that wants to be the best. Measuring sticks must be put in place, guidelines by which the group can compare itself to its peers.

3. Competition in itself may not be sufficient, you may just wind up being the best of the lousiest. So other guidelines are necessary, such things as goals and "purpose." There must be an effort to reflect issues as well as financial success: Teamwork, community worth, futures.

4. With every tool available, our Man must motivate. Neither goals, purposes or competitions mean a damned thing unless he makes it exciting, fun and important. More than

anything else, people must really want to work. Spoon feeding, meetings, rallies, private conferences, rewards, recognition, praise, ass-kicking; which of these would you eliminate if you desperately wanted to succeed?

***Webster* on *"Teamwork"*:** *Cooperative or coordinated effort on the part of a group of persons acting together as a team or in the interests of a common cause.*

I couldn't have said it better.

HUSTLE, NOT NECESSARILY A STREET WORD

FOR BASEBALL PLAYERS the word "hustle" refers to a special kind of horseplay called "pepper." A player, the instigator, hustles his team by shouting encouraging remarks and razzing the other team, sometimes calling their batters "bums," and in general "peppering" the air with enthusiasm and excitement. One player, famous for his highly bombastic style of "pepper," wrote about it in a best seller titled, "How I raised Myself From Failure To Success Through Enthusiasm." Too long ago to remember his name.

The word "hustle" is also street language for pushing things you're not supposed to, like drugs, stolen merchandise, phony "name" brand watches and other contraband. The most common use of the word refers to the sale of personal favors by "loose" women, or "hustlers."

In the business world, "Hustle," can be a verb or a complimentary adjective. The verb "to hustle" means to do what you do with great energy and intent. There's nothing nicer you can say about an employee, especially a salesman than, "He's a real hustler." The flip side of which is "dragging ass."

Hustling is a difficult trait to develop — unless it's inherent, you can only get there by setting examples. Only exposure to hustle can create hustle, so you need at least one role model. If you want hustlers, you either have to be one yourself and show the way or hire one and let them do it for you.

Hustlers can't help hustling, it's their thing. Others need role models or they haven't a clue.

Hustle itself isn't motivation; it's a result of motivation, and though hustlers are motivating to be around, it doesn't matter much to them as they pay little attention to anyone. If watching them function motivates you, then it's a start toward being one yourself. Hustlers have an inner motivation and an excitement for what they're doing; wonderful to be exposed to, but a tough act to follow.

Everything comes to those who hustle while they wait. *... Thomas Edison*

And for those that wouldn't know a hustler if they had just sold you the Brooklyn Bridge, here is a short course in "hustler" identification:

1. You never have to tell them to do anything twice, at times, not even once.
2. Whatever they're going to do, they do it NOW when later would be fine.
3. They have an intense desire to sell things or ideas to ... everyone.
4. They exude energy and create "motion," lots of motion, sometimes, without even moving.
5. Always the first to volunteer for anything! Hustlers are top-notch brown-nosers.
6. If there's any around, you'll know it. Whether you like it is something else.
7. They win contests, make goals, are success-oriented and are usually loud.

Hustlers make the rest of us look a little sluggish,

and though I love them, exposure over an extended period can be nerve-racking. In fact, for the long haul, they tend to be a pain in the ass, especially if you're competing with one.

In conclusion, no one will argue that business calls for hustle and it would be nice if everyone had a little of it. If you're short on this week's payroll, it's the "hustlers" that will go get it for you.

> ***Webster*** *on **"hustle,"** is fairly complete: To proceed or work rapidly, energetically. To push or force one's way. To be aggressive, especially in business. To earn one's living by illicit or unethical means. To solicit as a prostitute. To sell by high pressure tactics. To urge, prod or speed up. To beg or ask for money. To cheat or swindle.*

No one's perfect.

GREAT EXPECTATIONS

How MUCH of what you consider to be yours, belongings, success, satisfied dreams, or emotional stability, has come to you without great effort? Probably damned little. Worked your little tushy off, you did. On the other hand, that which you could have done without beautifully has probably poured in from every side without a word for the asking: measles, mumps, the flu, dental bills, Dear John letters, etc.

The latter part, referred to curiously as the maturing process, is assisted generously by a few independent agencies that are constantly making sure you receive your proper share of life's realities: draft notices, evictions, parking tickets, etc. At times, to convince you further of their intentions, they repossess your car and/or cancel your life insurance. This is all part of the aging metamorphosis which peaks when the IRS, at your death, without investing a cent, declares themselves an equal partner. Thinking about these things, and it's difficult not to, makes revolutions easier to understand.

If any of this comes as a surprise, I wonder what we've been thinking about?

Don't expect anything original from an echo ...?

To counter attack, we must condition ourselves and those

around that it is perfectly normal to expect good things from our life or our work. The not-so-good things will arrive unsolicited and on time.

Within reason, what can we actually expect from those around us, what kind of attitudes, performance standards, gratitude's, loyalties, affection ? And to what degree? Books filled with methods and philosophies designed to pull these qualities from people abound and can be very effective, especially if written in understandable English.

After reading a few of these, I find that although covering a multitude of ideas," expectations" are never fully defined. "Expectations" are treated as back burner stuff. There's all the advice you need on what you may want from people, but not what you to expect. In short, they're long on what to look for, but short on how to get it, which, considering the complexities, is easily understood.

There's a mystique about "expectations." Ordinarily we function in business by telling others what to do, and then with the use of tracking devices find out whether or not they do it. "Expecting" things from people puts the process in a different light.

Let's play a game. You're an employee and your boss says to you, "Schlomoe (because that's your name), here's what I want you to do." Then he tells you what he wants you to do and you set about doing it, or not doing it, depending on the kind of employee you are. In the end, you hope to go back to your boss with the results he wanted. Whether or not he remembers what it was may be the problem.

Instead, let's say the boss says, "Schlomoe, here's what I expect you to do." Wow! Don't tell me Schlomoe would feel the same about it. No way. There's one helluva difference in his wanting you to do something and "expecting" you to do something.

What's the point? In my humble opinion, we've been going about the business of leading — being a boss, a little vaguely. We train, we instruct, we practice, we drill and, in our own way, impart to our people what it is we want them to do. What we don't do, however, is give them a strong sense of what is expected of them.

But aren't wanting to and expecting to the same thing? No.

What I want you to do means "trying"; what I expect you to do means succeeding!

Unfortunately, it isn't as simple as exchanging the word "want" for the word, "expect." The change involves your philosophy which must move from: WORKING TOWARD AN END YOU WANT TO WORKING TOWARD AN END YOU EXPECT. As each of us learns differently, how one makes the change will vary from person to person.

The attitudes surrounding us will undoubtedly reflect our own; if we change our own, it will change theirs. Once we start expecting things to get done, the rest will fall in line.

There are two ways of spreading light: be the candle, or the mirror that reflects it.
... Edith Wharton

IT'S A WONDERFUL WHIRL

So, WHAT have we learned? "We" being the writer's way of saying "me." Putting it more clearly then, what have me learned?

For one thing, that which I jest about isn't necessarily that which I consider funny, For the most part, applied humor is a not-too-clever means of treating subjects I would rather not talk about, such as not paying employees adequately, not permitting people to express themselves freely, talking too bloody much myself, etc., etc. Until we can approach these topics openly, like: "You're really a cheap bastard" — "God, you have a big mouth" — "Stuff a sock in it," — making light of them is nothing but a bad dodge.

I'm also more convinced than ever that a talent for leadership, like a talent for closing sales, is inherent, that acquisition of these talents by outside means is difficult to impossible. Can one become an adequate leader without being born to it — of course. Can you become a great leader — I don't think so.

About "humor" — if it hasn't occurred to you that leadership as a profession is more or less hilarious, then you're not doing the same things I'm doing. If you can't see yourself as occasionally laughable, then God help you.

Enjoying other people's mistakes is damned rude. Laughing at your own, is soul saving.

What we've been looking at are the inner workings, or lack of them, of the leadership mind — the executive equation as viewed from ground level. It was very satisfactory to discover how much more intent we are to be better, different and more effective. Actually, we're not a bad bunch, one might even get to like us.

In putting these thoughts to paper, I've learned more about my own inadequacies than I care to discuss, but I have also learned quite pleasantly that I am more versed on the subject than I thought.

It's important to realize that these have been my thoughts, not yours, and as such they are second-hand and automatically suspect ... like a used car, you might say. If the reader took each chapter title and wrote their own version of it, they would then see the subject matter through their eyes and not someone else's and be better suited to train others, which in business is the end game.

Nothing can be taken for granted, certainly not someone else's theories.